Breaking Your Bonds

Finding Freedom Through Adversity

Catherine Carr

Stella Luma Press

Contents

For Those in Need

Suicide Hotline (US): 988

Samaritans Help Line (UK): 116-123

Crisis Text Line (US): Text SHOUT to 741-741

Crisis Text Line (UK): Text SHOUT to 85258

National Domestic Violence Hotline (US): 800-799-7233

Refuge's National Domestic Abuse Hotline (UK): 0808-2000-247

Also by Catherine Carr

*World Soul: Healing Ourselves and the
Earth Through Pagan Theology*

Content Advisory

This book contains discussions of trauma and exercises which may be triggering for some people.

It also contains descriptions of alcohol. Not that I drink much of it, but alcohol is used in many traditional religious ceremonies, and sometimes there's, um, a lot of it.

Disclaimer

The author takes no responsibility for the actions of readers of this book or their outcomes.

Readers are responsible for their own actions, and must use their own best judgment when it comes to their own health, safety, and finances.

The author makes no guarantees about the results of specific actions readers might choose to take after reading this book.

Please proceed with care.

Moving forward requires courage, but survival requires caution.

Please ensure you have some sort of safety net in place before you take a leap.

Introduction

E ight years ago, I performed my first Breaking of Bonds ritual alone in my apartment. It was a simple ritual that I now recognize as a type of cord-cutting, but its effects were staggeringly powerful. A year later I was traveling the country, working in an entirely different career. I'd sold my first short stories and articles, and won my first writing award. Things that I had not believed could change in my life *had* changed. Really, everything had.

You may not need everything in your life to change. Maybe it's only a small thing: a fear or habit you want to get rid of, a relationship you want to dissolve or change. Or maybe you do need a fresh start. That is for you to decide. My role here is to give you the best tools I can to do it.

The subtitle of this book is "Finding Freedom *Through* Adversity," not "Finding Freedom *Despite* Adversity," because it is my belief that I have the freedom I have now *because* I have encountered difficulties in my life. I have not had ease, but the necessity of working through obstacles has left me with the skills to make a way when the established roads are closed.

Here you will find:

- Discussion of the divine allies who teach us to protect ourselves, and to make the difference we are meant to make in the world.

- Discussion of best practices for consent, boundaries, and autonomy which can help us to create freedom for ourselves and others.

- Exercises to befriend your body and soul for purposes of healing and discernment.

- Exercises to get to know yourself, which might sound silly, unless you are like I was and have at some point told your therapist that you don't *know* what *you* want because you find it so unbearable to think about letting other people down.

- Procedures for the same ritual I performed, and information about the online-based community rituals and support groups I run.

Now, let me tell you a little bit more about myself so you'll know where I'm coming from.

In the weeks before my first ritual, I'd had something of a breakdown where I'd realized nothing in my life was working. People were coming to me seeking support because they knew I'd come through, but they didn't seem able to offer the same kind of support to me in return. The number of people saying they depended on me had reached a point where it was interfering with my career, and my career wasn't working either.

I'd been passed over for a promotion at work in favor of someone I'd trained. I subsequently realized that I didn't even *want* to advance on the current career path I'd been on for nine years. To top it all off, I was in a community and social group that almost unanimously disapproved of my religion, which was a bit of a problem because the sensation that my religion was my calling in life was getting stronger, not going away, as I got older.

I share all of this with you in case you see yourself in it. I had certainly never heard a story like my own growing up, and it was only the desperation of realizing that I wasn't happy with *any* of the paths I had imagined myself walking prompted me to try something new.

This, it turns out, is how new paths are made. By misfits who refuse to walk the existing ones. Now I work with a bunch of misfits who are *also* creating things that didn't exist before. It turns out there are thousands and thousands of us, and some of us are creating entire cultures of doing things that I was told were impossible growing up.

I also want to take a moment to speak about gods here.

I will speak about mine. Extensively. I initially wanted to write a version of this book which was friendly to all audiences, since I believe everyone can benefit from the principles presented here. But, I soon found that this book could not exist without detailed accounts of my work with trickster gods. They were such a powerful, and transformative, influence on my life that it was impossible to accurately chronicle my own liberation without them.

You may not work with gods. You may see all such things as psychological constructs, or you may work with only one God, or you may work with ancestors, angels, natural energies, or living humans as your mentors and supporters.

Unlike monotheists, Pagans don't tend to insist that our gods are *necessary* to the process of fulfillment and spiritual growth. Being polytheistic precludes the idea that our god is the only or best god or path there is. If there is more than one god, more than one legitimate tradition, then it's downright rude to insist that somebody follow yours in particular. So nobody is going to condemn you or call you inadequate because you don't work with gods (at least, nobody who is very knowledgeable on the subject).

But I will speak about gods, because our gods are, in many cases, the best mentors and supporters we have known. They are the influences who are both ancient and ever-new, who are not limited by the humans around us, or by any government or church (despite the best efforts of many governments and churches). This is why many modern people turn to Paganism: its gods embrace the people who the churches and governments reject.

So come with me, and let us learn about our allies, ourselves, and our power.

Chapter One

The Dark Allies of the Powerless

The rum splatters on the concrete around me, poured in a thick stream from the bottle taken from the altar. The one who's pouring it is Papa Legba, currently incarnate in the form of Mambo Jae Marie. He walks around me in a circle, saturating the pavement around me on all sides. Then, he points at the circle of rum.

"This," he bellows, "is where you stand! You stand in the middle of bullshit. Why are you voluntarily taking bullshit? Stop taking bull-shit!"

The lwa—spirits of Vodou—are nothing if not direct. I have indeed been feeling overwhelmed by stress for months, to the point of experiencing health problems as a result. If I am honest, much of my stress comes from things I have voluntarily agreed to. I know, in theory, that the problem is boundaries: I haven't been setting or enforcing sufficient ones; I have been remiss in training people to treat me the way I want to be treated.

A different god first taught me this lesson nine years ago: that the power and the choices are ultimately in my hands. That the costs of saying "no" may be high, but the cost of saying "yes" can be higher. Carving out the place you want in the world is possible, but one must guard one's own boundaries so rigorously in order to hold one's ground that it is easy to slip and fall.

"Get out of the bullshit!" Papa Legba shouts, pointing at the dry grass beside the circle of rum. I step out and he dumps rum *onto* me, soaking my trench coat. A profound blessing, I am told, and I wonder how I am going to explain this to my Lyft driver. "Now, don't go back!" he commands.

"You are hard-headed," he mutters then. But it's one of those affectionate mutters, the kind a grandparent uses when they recognize their own vice in you. Then he steps closer. "You need my love." And he embraces me warmly for a long time.

I needed the reminder. I've been taught the same lesson, exactly the same lesson, before. It took the better part of the last eight years for Loki to teach it to me, and to teach me how to change the world.

Our society does not like people who change the world, unless they are rich. It does not like people who question, who argue, who break rules. This might be less of a problem except that rules are often used to protect the powerful and oppress the powerless. One of the hardest lessons of my adult life has been learning how many of the rules that I was told existed to keep people safe were really designed to protect the powerful few.

This is what trickster gods like Loki and Papa Legba are for.

Trickster gods get a bad rap in the Abrahamic pantheon. "Trickster" invokes images of liars, of unethical behavior. Indeed, it's in the interest of empires and imperial religions to conflate "trickster" with "unethical." If we assume that the rules of society are right, after all, then breaking them can only be wrong.

Many people in the West struggle to understand why tricksters stand at the top of some indigenous pantheons, or are considered among their most important folk heroes. This is because the mainstream understanding of trickster gods ignores almost everything about what they actually do.

Tricksters subvert power. They revert to trickery, to that kind of intelligence that many cultures have called "cunning," to allow those without conventional power to triumph. It is tricksters who steal the powers the gods try to hoard for themselves and give them to humans.

Prometheus played the trickster when he stole fire from the gods and gave it to humanity. So did Innana when she used alcohol to wheedle the skills of civilization out of Enki, and gave them to the founders of humanity's first cities. In the book of Genesis in the Bible, the Serpent is called "deceiver" after he offers Eve the Fruit of Knowledge. But Yahweh never contradicts the Serpent's assertion that knowledge makes humanity like gods, and Adam and Eve do indeed appear to gain the knowledge of good and evil after they eat the fruit.

And it is knowledge that gives us the ability to create, to decide, to build a world with agency instead of simply accepting what is placed in front of us.

Tricksters do not fit the image of a glorious liberator, and that is good. If they did, they would become the "new boss, same as the old boss." Be wary of those who want to look good for the cameras. To play their role in creation, tricksters must remain dark, in the shadows, unacceptable.

Tricksters carve out space for the profane and unacceptable to be considered sacred because standards of "acceptability" are so often oppressive. By creating time and space to venerate the unacceptable, they create time and space to ask if current standards of acceptability are really right or good.

It's no wonder, then, that imperial religions don't like tricksters very much. But I do. And many people who feel powerless, who feel that society hasn't given them any leverage with which to change their world, find refuge in the friendship of trickster gods.

This book is not a trickster god devotional. I am not interested in getting you to profess devotion to, or develop a relationship with, any particular trickster god. But I want to introduce you to them, in case maybe they can help you.

Trickster gods are the ones who, since time immemorial, have guarded the door between life and death, between good and evil. They are the ones who have created norms and then destroyed them to make way for new norms, allowing progress. They are the ones who take everything that is dark, rejected, and unacceptable ,and make us see the beauty and the sacred in it. This includes ourselves.

So where do we begin on a journey of liberation?

Let us begin in the only place I know well enough to show you, which is the beginning of my own journey.

***

I was handed a spectacularly mixed deck of cards when I came into the world. My family was white and apparently upper-middle-class. I say "apparently" because my ancestors were mostly immigrant farmers and nomads who had been starved into assimilation and finally into flight by invading empires, and I am still unwrapping the layers of violent generational trauma stretching back to the colonization of Europe's wild lands.

My family internalized Christianization *hard*, which meant that I grew up under the guidance of conservative Christian churches. This was unfortunate, because teachers and members of those churches often used Biblical teachings to justify abusive behaviors, and demonized ideas which were actually helpful and liberating as "demonic" and "selfish."

For me, the most acute effect of being raised under conservative Christianity was that the divine contacts I had pretty much since birth were immediately squashed. I had always had religious experiences, which made me religiously devout. For me, the question of the Divine was never one of abstraction or obedience: I could actually see and feel what the priests and theologians were talking about, and I quite agreed that profound benefit could be obtained from spiritual practice and from cultivating certain kinds of discipline.

But as I grew, it turned out that none of my religious experiences were theologically correct according to my parents' church. Fortunately, I somehow managed to avoid internalizing the terror of Hell, and the sense of unworthiness that many of my peers developed in this environment.

Well, maybe I didn't avoid them completely. The guilt collided with some of the church's more humanitarian teachings, and I *did* develop a crippling sense that it was my job to say "yes" to anyone who asked me for anything. And to solve any problems I became aware of, whether they were my problems or not. And to make sure that nobody around me did anything unsafe or unwise, because I was, at some level, my brother's keeper.

At the time, this seemed like a good idea. The church had taught me that there was only one "right" way to do things, and that anyone who did anything otherwise was in grave danger of having their life ruined forever. I internalized the idea that I absolutely had to make all the safe and "right" decisions at all times if I wanted to have a roof over my head as an adult.

This was not helped at all by the global economic collapse of 2011, which happened almost the instant I became a legal adult. My home state lost hundreds of thousands of jobs and my family business went bankrupt. When I graduated after taking out student loans to make my degree possible, I found myself facing the worst national job market in 60-90 years (depending on which economist you ask).

I could spend a lot of time explaining the complications of those years, from the profound loss of support that happened when I left the church I grew up in, to the months I spent getting laughed out of interviews for waitressing jobs for being overqualified. And maybe I will address those stories someday, because even back then I was being taught quiet lessons about how getting fed up to the point of refusing to do as I was told got more done than actually playing by the rules.

But I think you get it. I've been through the ringer in some weird ways.

I've titled this book "Finding Freedom *Through* Adversity," instead of "Finding Freedom *From* Adversity" for a very important reason.

If I had not experienced any of those hardships, I would be totally at the mercy of the systems of power that prevail in our society. If I had been given wealth, I would have spent my life at the mercy of those who gave it to me. If I had lucked into a high-paying job right out of college, I would have spent my life at the mercy of employers.

If I had stayed in good standing with my church, or if I had never had the experience of having to *leave* a church which was my main source of community, I would be at the mercy of any community I might find myself in. I would rely on their approval and be, to some degree, trapped by the siren song of comfort.

I didn't have any of those opportunities. I never had a six-figure job to lose, so there was little standing in the way of my gods' lessons about priorities. I spent my first decade of adulthood enduring rejection by authority figures and the religious community I grew up in, so I have no fear of speaking truth to power. I found the mentor who helped me build the businesses I run today by joining a protest movement out of rage when no employer would take me after eight months and eighty job applications.

If I had not had my adversity, I would not be free.

Let's now see what freedom we can build for you.

Chapter Two

The Beginning of Sovereignty

There was a time when I was not a big fan of the idea of personal sovereignty.

Under the kind of "one right wayism" preached by some religions and other moralistic ideologies people believe that we *know* what the right way to do things is. As such, everything else is secondary; individuals' consent, boundaries, and autonomy don't really need to be considered, because if those individuals want to do the right thing, they will agree with the authority figure. And if they don't, then they're being sinful or harmful and no one is obliged to do what they want.

This is what I was taught: that people are inherently flawed and sinful, and that talk of prioritizing consent, boundaries, autonomy, and individual desires was a symptom of a sinful, selfish culture which prioritized individual selfishness above The Right Thing To Do.

I now realize how toxic this framework was. Abusive behavior by men and authority figures was justified as either "discipline for the greater good" or "inevitable human sinfulness," while the normal, healthy desires of women and children were demonized as disobedience to God. Any vocation or calling which was not approved by the church was characterized as "confusion" at best, and then as "evil" if attempts at "correction" did not dissuade a person from their path.

This does not only happen in churches. Similar dynamics can be found in many families and workplaces, where those in power might characterize *their* needs, desires, and beliefs as being "for the greater good" or "perfectly justified" while the needs and ideas of others are portrayed as incorrect, flawed, weak, immoral, etc..

Does this sound familiar to you?

This sort of dynamic is so common in our society that most people enter adulthood not believing that they deserve to be treated well and not necessarily understanding how to treat others well either. This can manifest in everything from business and workplace negotiations to intimate and family relationships.

As such, we will spend the next few chapters of this book learning frameworks for how people treat each other in truly healthy situations, how to have some control over how others treat us, and how to heal from being treated poorly in the ways that "one right wayism" typically creates. In the process we will get a taste of how the darker gods can be our allies in self-defense, and how having experienced hardship in the first place can make us more effective at combating it.

To begin to defend ourselves, we must know what is "us" and what is not.

When I began my journey, I had very little sense of who I was, or of where I ended and others began. I was in fact *discouraged* from having a sense of myself, since it was assumed that "myself" would be inferior to God, or to whatever authority figure claimed to speak for him in the moment. The work of life was presented to me as the work of complete self-sacrifice in which I lived to serve God's will and not my own.

I did not know, at that time, that there was a philosophy within which all humans, and indeed all living beings, *contain* sparks of God which are meant to manifest in the world in unique ways. This sort of pantheism was rejected as heresy by my church for reasons that aren't hard to understand: the decentralized God, made each individual human a legitimate carrier of Divine will and revelation. This made it considerably harder to claim that some people had the divine right to tell others what to do and "discipline" them into doing it.

Under the influence of the philosophy of ultimate self-sacrifice, I became one of those people who absorbed the emotions of everybody I saw like a sponge. I felt other people's distress almost as acutely as they did. That might not have been a problem, except that the result was to leave me powerless. I felt powerless to disagree with anyone, powerless to say "no" to them, powerless to cause them even temporary distress.

The problem with being completely sensitive to other people's distress is that it turns out distress is not just a product of evil oppression, but also a necessity for learning, growth, and change. Nobody teaches most people in our society to differentiate between those causes of distress, and this leads to tremendous amounts of harm in at least two different ways.

In my case, I became a problem-solver from an early age. As early as kindergarten, I noticed when classmates were being mistreated, and learned almost immediately that adults would not necessarily solve these problems, and would often make it worse. So it was up to me to solve them.

This all worked very well for a while, but by the time I started attending therapy seriously in my mid-20s, I had absolutely no sense of self outside of my ability to solve problems for other people. My therapist asked me what I wanted out of life, and I couldn't tell him. I could only tell him what my friends needed, what my parents needed, and how I absolutely did not have time to even think about what *I* wanted because those people had so many needs.

Does this sound familiar to anybody? In my mid-20s, I was just figuring out that this whole situation was not sustainable, and was not creating long-term solutions to any problems.

My therapist was the first human to suggest to me that I actually needed to be aware of my own desires to be a healthy person. He was the first human to suggest to me that I was not obligated to solve other people's problems, and have me take him seriously.

I specify "human" for reasons we'll get into later. For now, if we're going to talk about sovereignty, we've first got to figure out how you can recognize what is "you" and what is "not you." This may prove harder than you expect.

The ABCs of Autonomy, Boundaries, and Consent

When I was first drafting this book, I had the impulse to cover autonomy, boundaries, and consent in a convenient alphabetical order. However, I soon realized it had to be done exactly the opposite way. This is because the easiest access point to separating yourself from others was the point of consent.

The question "will you consent to this" is a single, clear decision point—a clear moment illuminating the nature and boundaries of your person. When someone asks "may I hug you?" or "would you like to do this?" that's an invitation to sense your own genuine desires and emotions.

We may not always read it that way, especially if we have been raised in a culture where it is not acceptable for us to say "no." But questions like these, moments like these where we are *asked* what we want, are still the easiest access point to begin to ask who *we* are when we are not worrying about displeasing somebody or solving somebody's problems.

We can think of these opportunities as single data points on a 3D grid which paint a picture of ourselves. Every true emotion we uncover when we are asked "would you like this?" or "do you want this?" shows us a tiny piece of ourselves.

Once we have collected enough data points, we can begin to get an idea of where our boundaries lie. Consent is a single decision point. Boundaries are more general policies for how we deal with entire categories of situations. Autonomy is what happens when these boundaries are enforced and you are able to live freely, not beholden to pathological guilt or fear.

In recent years, mainstream society's education about autonomy, boundaries, and consent has gotten better. And by "better" I mean that most people I speak to now have at least heard of these concepts.

When I was growing up, I hadn't really. Right and wrong was reckoned Biblically; what your goals "should" be was dictated by society, and what you "should" want to do in any given situation was dictated by those goals. People who chose something different from those goals were considered weak or failures, and people who spoke of their own needs were considered weak or selfish.

Even now, discussions of autonomy, boundaries, and consent do not guarantee that they are actually being respected. More than once, I've known someone who lectured me about boundaries—when *other* people wanted things from me, and their needs took my time and attention away from the lecturer. These same people who encouraged me to "learn about boundaries," when it came to *other* people, were often the first to tell me I was being cruel and unreasonable when I did not give in to *their* desires.

That sort of rhetoric can be damaging precisely because it is confusing; a person can be convinced that their relationship partner must be great because they use all the right "therapy speak," yet still be left feeling like they've done something wrong every time they do what makes them happy. It's actually easy to convince someone that they are the problem when you can pay lip service to enlightened ideals.

So let's start from scratch, shall we? Let's assume that you haven't heard about these concepts before.

Consent

Let us start with consent, because it's the easiest to explain. It's also a staggeringly powerful moral framework that can improve ethics in everything from personal relationships to some of the most contentious issues facing our societies.

The idea of consent is quite simple: does someone agree to have something happen to them? Do they agree to being touched, to being treated in a certain way, to fulfilling certain duties in a relationship? Do they agree to undertake a certain activity or to receive a certain medical treatment?

Does the person agree? Do they want this?

It's as simple as that.

When consent is used as a major determiner of what is right and what is wrong, the world opens.

When consent is considered sacrosanct, there is precious little room for argument about whether someone's boundaries are "reasonable." There is no imperative for anyone to tolerate being treated in ways they don't want to be treated, because the question of "how should you treat other people?" is answered with "the way they tell you they want to be treated."

Consent, when used as a basis for morality, effectively replaces the flawed and imperfect unspoken rules which, in so many cultures, define the types of treatment that various people are considered entitled to, or are expected to endure. In consent culture, the question is no longer "is it reasonable for you to want to be treated better?" The answer is always "you deserve people who will treat you the way you want to be treated."

Some of you may already see the makings of a conflict. What if someone's demand is to be treated *better* than the way others are treated? What if someone's demand is, for example, total obedience from other people?

Well, people are welcome to demand that, to consent to relationships only on those terms. And other people are free *not* to consent to those terms, and to be in relationship with other people.

Consent, as something that is required from every person equally, is a great equalizer. Powerful people cannot get away with abuses in societies where consent is the gold standard for how things must be done. Those who may be considered to be at the bottom of the social hierarchy, in terms of measures like fame and fortune, are just as entitled to have their consent, or lack thereof, respected as anyone else.

You may think this is a somewhat utopian vision I describe. And in some ways, it is; consent culture has made disturbingly little progress in penetrating mainstream culture so far, with most modern people still harkening to cultural expectations about what is considered "normal" to guide their behavior and their expectations about what is possible for them. Peer pressure and toxic relationship expectations are still all too common, with too many people feeling that they'll be ostracized, or somehow in the wrong, if they express their true desires for how they wish to be treated.

But consent culture is also a reality being lived by a growing number of people each year. In a growing number of social circles, relationships are explicitly negotiated by people who know exactly what they need and are seeking in a relationship, instead of being governed by unspoken societal norms.

In these social circles, it is often considered necessary to ask consent for things that might be assumed to be acceptable by the prevailing culture. Some may require that a person ask consent for *any* physical touch, to avoid accidentally triggering someone or making them uncomfortable. Some may advise obtaining consent before engaging in certain types of conversations.

While those who are not used to these conversations may find these expectations unreasonable, or even absurd, they are actually very easy to practice. It's as simple as asking, "Would you like a hug?" "Can I hold your hand?" or "Are you in a good place to talk about _____ right now?"

It's not difficult. And it's incredibly liberating. It is especially liberating for people who have lived in fear of saying "no," or in fear that they will be rejected if they express their true preferences or desires. It is especially liberating for people who have lived in fear of letting people get close to them at all, assuming that being close to someone will mean having their wishes disregarded.

And that is the endgame of this Bond Breaking work. It is not about isolation: it is about breaking *unhealthy* bonds and expectations to make room for new, better, healthier versions. Nothing new can grow in a forest clogged by underbrush, after all, and tricksters must destroy the old order before they can create a better new one.

Many people have complained that consent culture limits them by increasing the number of things they have to ask others for permission to do. This can be especially frustrating for people who are powerful or privileged in the old order, who are used to living under the assumption that they can do as they please, and people can't, or won't, say "no" to them.

But another benefit of consent culture is this: it dramatically *expands* the range of possibilities for everyone.

In a consent culture that actually practices its principles, you are not hemmed in by the definitions of what is "normal" and the fear that others will be angry or reject you if you propose something that is outside the norm.

Instead, consent culture allows a person to propose or request nearly anything they want; since the understanding is that it is okay to say "no" to any proposal for any reason, a request is treated less like an oppressive expectation that someone is imposing on another, and more like a possibility that they're exploring.

Similarly, the risk of agreeing to try something new is lessened: in consent culture, you know that you can ask for whatever safety measures you may desire when trying something new, and you know that if you ask someone to stop and they *don't,* there is a good chance they will face serious social repercussions.

In consent culture, victim-blaming is much more difficult because the question of whether the victim's actions or expectations were "normal" or "reasonable" does not come into play in a paradigm where "right" and "wrong" for any action is defined by whether consent was given.

Remember, we are not just talking about sex here. That is where many people's minds go immediately, but the same logic can be applied to any situation involving interactions between two people. Whether the interaction is verbal, physical, or some other type of interaction, consent culture protocols can be applied when asking for what you want and when asking for it to stop when you're not comfortable.

And yes, this really does happen. As consent culture slowly filters into mainstream culture, it has in fact become more difficult for the powerful to commit abuses, and easier for victims to find support. There is a long way to go yet, but the progress that has happened in my lifetime so far has been astonishing.

It has been especially astonishing for me as someone who moved from a conservative Christian culture, where girls were told to assume that men would not be able to control themselves if we showed too much skin, and that intimate relationships demanded a mindset of service and sacrifice from us by default, into a far left consent culture as an adult.

I sometimes like to say I've done "six impossible things before breakfast," because things really are possible in consent culture that conservatives often claim are literally not possible, because they feel it is not reasonable to expect human beings to behave so respectfully and supportively toward each other.

Now, I wanted to give you an idea of the power of consent before getting into the technical details. But the technical details are *important*. The basis of consent is saying "yes, I want this," or "no, I do not agree to this." But there are several attributes that consent should have to be valid.

I'm going to use a favorite acronym of mine here: CRISP, developed by Intimacy Directors and Coordinators (it might interest you to know that these are the folks who became famous working on love scenes in the Netflix Bridgerton series). While the CRISP acronym is designed for actors working in the performing arts, I like it better than Planned Parenthood's FRIES acronym for a few reasons I'll discuss shortly.

One is that the IDC's CRISP requirements for consent are actually quite similar to the elements of informed consent I learned as a research coordinator inviting people to participate in clinical research, but they are easier to remember and worded in a way that's friendlier and less clinical. Here I'll give both the IDC's take on CRISP, and a corresponding example from my clinical research career.

According to CRISP requirements, valid consent should be:

- Considered. This means the person can take time to consider whether to consent or not if they want to. Consent should never be forced to rush or decide "right now." In fact, when I worked in emergency medicine research there was an understanding that it was inherently impossible to obtain informed consent when a decision was needed literally ASAP, and there was a whole different set of decision-making protocols we used to protect individuals and the community in situations where there was no time for the patient to consider their wishes in the moment.

- Reversible. This means that if you consent to something but then change your mind or find it not to your liking, you can withdraw consent at any time. This means the other person has to respect it if you want to stop. In the clinical research world, this means that a patient can withdraw from the research study at any time, and not be prevented from stopping or punished for doing so. The same applies to consent in relationships.

- Informed. This means that you know what you are agreeing to, including any potential benefits or risks. In clinical research, scientists are required to disclose all possible risks of participating in the research study for consent to be valid.

In a relationship this might mean that you have the right to research and ask about the risks of an activity you're considering undertaking, and that ideally the person proposing the activity should inform you of these. Since most people you engage in relationships with are not research scientists who keep a list of documented clinical risks on hand, though, it's probably a good idea to do your own research if the activity you're considering seems potentially risky.

- Specific. This means that you agree to do something specific, and the other person has no right to assume that you are *also* agreeing to other things you haven't discussed. In clinical research, we couldn't perform *any* research procedures on subjects that they did not *specifically* agree to. We weren't allowed to say "but you said you want to help with research, so we assumed you'd be fine with this other research procedure that we didn't specifically ask about too."

- Participatory. This means that you should be involved in the process of deciding what you are agreeing to as much as possible. In some consent culture circles, "consent and participation" is considered a gold standard for demonstrating consent, since if someone is passively sitting back letting other people make all the decisions it may be possible that they don't feel comfortable speaking up.[1]

---

1. Coordinators, I. D. &. (2022, October 25). *Defining consent: From fries to crisp!*. Intimacy Directors and Coordinators. https://idcprofessionals.com/blog/defining-consent-from-fries-to-crisp

In clinical care, this can refer to the fact that a patient should be consulted about which of the available treatment options they want to take, and should ideally ask questions and state preferences. This is not a burden that is placed on the patient or the person giving consent, but rather is a way for the people obtaining the consent to gauge if the person is truly comfortable speaking up and expressing their preferences. In my clinical research career, it was recommended that we use the phrase "what questions do you have?" instead of "do you have any questions?" This was because of concern that someone answering "no" to the question "do you have any questions" might not have been paying attention to important information about their health and safety.

That may all sound like a lot, and indeed it is probably not necessary to go through this framework step by step every time you ask someone if they'd like a hug. But if you find yourself in doubt as to whether it is "reasonable" for you to be upset that someone has done something that violated your boundaries or tried to coerce you into doing something you don't want to do, you may wish to consult this acronym to remind you what really good consent should look like.

Of note, many people also like Planned Parenthood's FRIES acronym for discussing sexual consent. I chose not to use that one because many people feel that the "enthusiastic" part of that framework is limiting and might prevent people from exploring things they're uncertain about. Some also have concerns that the definition of "freely given" might be vague. But I invite you to investigate FRIES and see if it's helpful to you as well.

Now that we've looked at what really good consent should look like, let's think about how adopting a consent culture worldview could change your life.

What would it mean if you knew you had a right to be treated as you wish to be treated, and that your boundaries and desires aren't "unreasonable?" What would it mean if you knew that there *are* people who would treat you that way, and that you just have to find them?

What are situations in your life right now that you did *not* consent to?

What are situations in your life right now that you *do* consent to?

What are situations that you would *like* to consent to, if you had the opportunity?

Allow yourself to fantasize about what is possible for you. Dreaming and wishing is the first step of all magic. A thing cannot be created until it has first been fully imagined.

I will leave you to ponder that for a while.

***

Activity 1: Consent Worksheet

It can be difficult to express what we do and don't want if no one ever asks for our opinion or permission. In this exercise, I want you to create some hypotheticals so you will get some practice saying "yes" and "no" and see what that feels like.

To start with, I'm going to ask you to formulate sentences in the following ways:

"Would you like to _____?"

"May I _____?"

Now, what are five "would you like to _____?" or "may I _____?" questions to which the answer is *yes*? What are five things you would *like* someone to invite you to do, or to offer to do for you?

1. Would you like to

_____ ?

2.

3.

4.

5.

Next, what are five "would you like to _____?" or "may I _____?" questions to which the answer is *no*? What are five things you do *not* like to do, or do not like people to do to you? You may wish to try thinking of things people *actually* do which bother you, so that you can get practice saying "no" to these things.

1. May I

_____ ?

2.

3.

4.

5.

Now, since people often don't ask your preferences or permission, let's formulate five ways to say "no" to the things you *don't* want in your life.

1. Please don't

_____.

2. If you _____,
   I'm going to leave.

3. If you _____, I'm going to
   hang up the phone.

4. I   can't

_____

right now.

5. I   don't   want   to
_____ right now.

Of note, if you have had difficulty finding answers for the blanks above, I strongly urge you to seek mental health treatment as soon as possible. If you are unable to say what you do or don't want, if you are unable to say what makes you feel good or bad, there is a high likelihood that you are dealing with a trauma or mental illness which is having a strong effect on your nervous system.[2]

It is difficult to recover from such a thing without strong support, so enlisting the help of a mental health professional is a very good idea. If no mental health professional is available, you may wish to investigate local groups in your area such as support groups or online communities who may be able to help.

Now, there's one last exercise I would like to do. I want you to practice saying "no" in the mirror.

_____

2. A., V. der K. B. (2015). _The Body Keeps the Score: Brain, Mind, and Body in the Healing of Trauma_. Penguin Books.

When people don't respect your "no," it is often necessary to escalate. This can feel difficult for some of us who are accustomed to being ignored or punished for saying "no." For that reason, actually practicing, physically and out loud, can have beneficial effects. It can create muscle memory and neural pathways that we can draw on when a real-world situation calls for us to say "no."

Let's try practicing three types of "no"s:

1. The kind and gentle "no, thank you." This can sometimes be an appropriate place to start, and can be just as liberating as an aggressive "no" if we are not used to feeling that we have the option to say "no" at all. Practice saying, "Oh, no thank you," to yourself in the mirror five times.

2. The firm, "I said, no." This sometimes becomes necessary when people disregard your first refusal of consent. Know that anybody who disregards your refusal of consent at any time is showing bad behavior, and is probably not going to be the most trustworthy or supportive person in your life. Practice saying, "I said, no," to yourself in the mirror five times.

3. For our final escalation, there is the loud, disgusted, "No!" This is the "no" that gets people's attention in public places and alerts them that something is wrong. Whether you've merely been insulted or are being threatened, if someone hears a loud "no!" in a public place their ears are likely to perk up and eyes are likely to turn toward you. Practice saying a loud, enthusiastic "no!" in the mirror to yourself five times.

How did that feel?

For our final exercise, let's imagine what is possible for you. Remember those questions from the first exercise, about invitations and offers you'd *like* to say "yes" to?

Take those five questions, and write responses to them below. You might begin with something like, "Yes, I'd like to _____." Say exactly what it is that you would *like* to do out loud. In magic, words have power. To get what you want most, you must first identify what you really want and ask for it. As in medicine, it is necessary to know what your goals are before you can make choices that help you to meet them:

1. Yes, I would like to

_____.

2. Yes, I would be honored to

_____.

3.

4.

5.

We are still in the earliest stages of magic, as I will explain next. But you have already opened up new neural pathways by practicing saying "no" to what you don't want, and voicing aloud the possibility of saying "yes" to what you do want. Over the next few days, watch and see how your life changes.

You may repeat these practice exercises as often as is helpful.

Chapter Three

Boundaries

"Boundaries" is a popular term in pop psychology these days. In my youth, I was told that I should "learn how to set boundaries" several times before anyone really explained to me what this meant.

So what is a boundary? In a literal sense, a boundary is a dividing line between two areas. It's a limit, and a border which must be guarded to preserve what lies within.

In international politics, of course, a border is where one nation's jurisdiction ends and another begins. Each nation, if truly free, is entitled to rule over what happens within its own borders. A free nation is entitled to control what happens within its own borders, and to decide how to use its own resources, and what rules it will live under, etc.. Generally speaking, one nation isn't allowed to police what goes on within another nation's borders, cross those borders without permission, or demand access to resources within the other nation's borders.

This is a good starting point for thinking about boundaries among people. A boundary is the boundary or border of your own person—beyond which you decide what happens. Boundaries can refer to who you allow to physically touch you and how, what kinds of conversations and exchanges you will participate in, and what kind of treatment you will tolerate from others, etc.. Properly used, boundaries ensure that you can flourish and thrive by protecting your well-being and the growth you are cultivating within yourself.

What is sometimes tricky about boundaries is understanding their enforcement. Obviously, we cannot simply *make* people treat us as we wish. People won't simply do what we say because we've said it, and it's improper on several levels to violate other people's boundaries or try to use force in an attempt to enforce our own. An invasion of someone else's boundaries because they violated your own is exactly what it sounds like: it's a war, in which there are no winners because both sides take damage, and neither is sovereign or free to flourish in the midst of combat.

The most common mechanisms for boundary enforcement involve removing oneself from the situation that you no longer wish to tolerate. This approach has the first and foremost effect of keeping *your* territory safe:; you can't be adversely affected by someone else's behavior if you're no longer around them. It can also serve as a consequence that gives others incentive to respect your wishes. If someone truly wishes to have you around, and respecting your boundaries is the only way for them to accomplish that, they are more likely to change their ways than if you allow them to ignore your boundaries without consequences.

Tricksters might seem an odd type of spirit to teach consent and boundaries. After all, they get their name from a penchant for playing pranks and making misleading statements. But this is another area where tricksters can offer a refreshing perspective.

Their take on consent is very practical: instead of teaching you a whole lot of theory about what consent should be like, they will teach you to defend yourself.

One of my most powerful memories of Loki is this:

I was crying in my bed one night, feeling absolutely desolate. I don't even remember why that was, now. It was a point where I was beginning to deal with the fallout of saying "no," of refusing to behave according to the expectations of people around me.

I wasn't in a good place. I had not yet realized that there were people in the world who would treat me better than I was accustomed to. I had not yet realized that I was actually doing some of these people a *disservice* by trying to solve their problems for them, instead of giving them consequences that could force them to grow and adapt.

And I was having trust issues. Whatever had happened on that night, it had come from someone I trusted, from someone who was not among the first to reject me when I began to grow and change. And I wondered: could I really trust anybody?

Loki appeared, all red hair and sharp cheekbones and unsettlingly green eyes. And I asked him: "What if *you* turn on me someday?"

He stared at me, eyes round with incredulity. In hindsight, I'm not sure which it was: incredulity that I thought that he would do that, or incredulity that I didn't already know what to do if he did.

Wordlessly, he reached for the knife in his belt.

And handed it to me.

No one had ever urged me to protect myself, even from *them*, before. No one had ever given me permission, let alone the means to do it.

That is what I mean when I say tricksters are refreshingly practical. If you ask them how to stop oppression, or how to protect yourself in a relationship, they will hand you a knife. All the high-minded idealism in the world is worth very little, after all, if there is no enforcement.

I believe this may also be one reason why, in my experience, people who come from adversity are particularly rigorous adherents of consent culture and other cultural innovations that are creating a better world. When a culture's expectations have caused one unbearable pain, one is less likely to accept cultural expectations unquestioningly in the future and more likely to set out to make something better.

Of course, most relationship partners aren't Loki, and stabbing is unlikely to improve most situations. But enforcing boundaries, even in the gentlest ways, can sometimes be treated as a violent act by people who aren't used to being forced to honor boundaries. I know I was sometimes accused of being cruel and hurtful in the early days of enforcing my own boundaries by people who couldn't handle the idea of me not doing what they wanted. So perhaps the metaphor of becoming comfortable with self-defense here is apt.

This is my segue into the question of how *you* enforce your boundaries.

In the previous chapter I described boundaries as being general policies for what you do and do not want in your life. Where consent happens at the point of specific possibilities and requests, boundaries attempt to project a hypothetical. "I will leave the room if you raise your voice at me." "I will hang up the phone if you begin talking about that."

A proper boundary contains its own consequence. Boundaries don't simply mean telling other people what they must do around you. When telling people what to do, after all, your options are as follows: either have zero enforcement mechanism, or try to force people to do your bidding. One is unlikely to be successful, the other is unlikely to be ethical.

But what you *can* do is decide what *you* will or will not tolerate. The most successful boundaries involve removing yourself from a situation if the boundary is violated. This is no dDraconian enforcement method—it is not denying anyone anything that is theirs by right, since no one is entitled to your time, attention, or company.

The sole exception to this is minors who you *made*, i.e. *your* minor children, who are in fact entitled to your care and labor since you are the one who brought them into existence. If you *are* a minor child, remember that: you don't have to repay your parents for keeping you alive. That is the job they signed up to do for eighteen years when they made you.

If you ever feel guilty for enforcing a boundary, you can take comfort in the fact that removing yourself from a situation is considerably kinder than stabbing somebody. You may even be doing the unhappy party a favor by illustrating that their actions have consequences, and they can only control their consequences by controlling their actions.

It is an interesting fact that this metaphor of truth as a blade is the reason why the suit of Swords in tarot is associated with both intellect and conflict; the "razor's edge of truth" is often perceived as rather cutting to those on the receiving end, but that doesn't mean it's wrong to use it. I affectionately refer to my Queen of Swords card, a card associated with both analytical thinking and clear boundaries, as "the bullshit slayer."

There is one more piece of magic I want you to know about here. The "Witches' Pyramid," is a traditional tool used to describe the essential elements of magic. Like the geometric structure of a pyramid, the Witch's Pyramid contains four corners, each of which are necessary to put in place before the magical apex can be reached. These are:

- Noscere (to know)

- Velle (to will)

- Audere (to dare)

- Ire (to go)[1]

The stage of this process which must come first is Noscere, "to know." The reason for this is obvious: nothing can be willed, or dared, or created, until it has first been discovered and envisioned.

No desire can be acted upon until you know you have it. No injury or illness can be healed until it has been diagnosed. No new world can be built until it has been envisioned, and the steps to get from here to there have been figured out.

It's like the serpent said. Knowledge is power.

So in these first few chapters, we are doing the work of Noscere. We are doing the work of determining what you want and what is harming you. Noscere is associated with the direction of the East, where the Sun comes up to start each new beginning and each new day. It is also associated with the element of air, and the tarot suit of Swords—the razor's edge of truth, the bullshit slayers.

This can be surprisingly challenging work. Those of us whose lives have been so filled with the needs of others that we have never had the chance to pay attention to our own desires might not know *what* we want, or what we feel called to manifest in the world. Those of us whose "yes" and "no" are not respected by the people around us may lose track of what feels good or bad to us, or even numb ourselves at a deep neurological level in order to avoid pain. Those of us who have been discouraged from dreaming "impossible" dreams or are repeatedly disappointed by life may not even know what we dream of anymore.

We are going to work on all of that here.

The consent exercises were the beginning of that. Answering a "yes" or "no" question is among the easiest of things to do. By listening to how different proposals feel in your body, you can get an idea of what you and your body really like and dislike. In my theology, this is actually a manifestation of Divine will; the spark of the Divine in us is most reliably understood from *inside* our nervous systems, not from external authorities as some religions teach. Boundaries are a next step in protecting and nurturing that Divine spark in you.

Boundaries are pro-active. Instead of waiting to be asked if something feels good or bad to you, boundaries allow you to make policies which allow you to step away from situations which aren't good for you when they arise. Boundaries empower you to leave situations that you may have felt trapped in before, and to know that the leaving is justified because your wishes and well-being aren't being respected in the situation.

We can think of boundaries as the protection of the borders of your internal territory. You are a sovereign nation; you get to choose what happens inside of your boundaries, and what doesn't. If any outside nation tries to police what is happening inside your boundaries, they are overstepping their rights according to international law. In many cases, attempts to forcibly change what is happening inside another country's boundaries is considered an act of war for good reason.

Let us take a few minutes here to consider what boundaries would help you to defend the borders of your being from outside interference.

What are five boundaries you would set in your life right now if you could? Remember that a boundary should include both a statement about what you will not accept, and a statement of how you are going to remove yourself from the situation if the behavior continues. Some examples might include:

- I will not work more hours than I'm paid for, so I won't

check my work emails after 6pm.

- I won't tolerate having my wishes ignored, so I will leave if you ignore my "no."

- I don't want to talk about this with you anymore, so I will hang up the phone if you insist on talking about it.

- I won't tolerate this person mistreating others, so I will leave if they start mistreating others while I am around.

-

What are four boundary statements you would like to make right now?

1.

2.

3.

4.

Are there any of these boundaries that feel feasible to implement right now? Are there any that feel unsafe in your current situation?

If you answered "yes" to the second question, what situations would you have to leave and replace with new situations in order to feel safe enforcing all your boundaries?

If you feel *physically* unsafe about the idea of enforcing any of these boundaries, it may be wise to research local shelters and hotlines for people in abusive situations. Sometimes having a place to go in an emergency can make a big difference. You may wish to search these questions using a private device like a password-locked phone, or a web browser in incognito mode, if you are concerned about someone discovering your search.

The work of leaving old situations and creating new ones is tremendous, which is why we are going to need to go through all the phases of the Witches' Pyramid before we can do it. But the first step, always, is *knowing* what needs to change and what we want to replace it with.

If there are any situations that you feel you need to leave in order to be able to safely enforce your boundaries, what sort of situations would you like to replace them with? Allow yourself to dream here. All great realities begin with dreams, and I promise you more is possible than you think if you have patience and are willing to learn and grow.

Specifically, for each situation that felt like you might need to change it to have your consent and boundaries respected, what would your *ideal* situation look like five years from now?

If you are young, five years might sound like a long time. It *is* long enough to build something you might currently believe is impossible, but it is not such a large part of your life that you can't afford to invest it. People spend four to eight years in professional schools all the time; with focused growth and action, you can make much greater changes than that in five years.

So in five years, in your wildest fantasies, where would you like to be in each of these areas of your life?

1. In the realm of career and finance, I would like to be:

2. In the realm of emotions and relationships, I would like to be:

3. In the realm of intellect and skill, I would like to be:

4. In the realm of passion and spirituality, I would like to be:

I am going to leave you to study each of these visions further, to dwell within them and see how they feel in your body. You may wish to use the Jungian art of "active imagination," speaking with the people you imagine in your visions to learn more about them, and more about who you are in this vision and how you got from where you are now to where you are in this future.

Chapter Four

Autonomy

The final concept in our "ABCs" had to come last, because it is the most difficult to explain from scratch. This is the concept of autonomy.

Autonomy refers to the right of a person to self-govern, and their ability to do so. An "autonomous" nation or territory is one that makes its own decisions about what laws to follow, how to use its resources, how to interact with other nations, etc.. Autonomy can be thought of as "a state of consent." It is what happens when people are able to truly freely choose how to live.

This is another term, like consent, that comes up a lot in medicine. "Bodily autonomy" refers to the idea that people have the right to decide what happens to their bodies. Doctors and scientists aren't allowed to insist on "what's best for them" or demand that their bodies be put to the service of the public good. I want to take a moment to discuss autonomy in medicine, because it's helpful to understanding what autonomy looks like and why it is, despite the protestations of some conservatives, a good thing.

The prioritizing of bodily autonomy in medicine represents a cultural evolution that's happened in the last few decades. For much of the 20th century, doctors and families could force people, especially women and children, to undergo medical treatments whether they wanted to or not.

The philosophy was that a person did not belong to themselves;: in many places under 20th century law, women and children literally *belonged* to their parents or husband, and parents and husbands often had the legal right to determine "what was best for a person" or "what would be best for the family."

Even when there was no family to be found, doctors themselves often felt a paternalistic sense of power and/or responsibility to their patients and society. In the 20th century, patients could be committed to involuntary treatment if a doctor felt that they were not making the "right" decisions about their care, or felt that they were a "danger" to society. People with "deviant" sexual behaviors were among those who could be deemed "dangers to society" by doctors and politicians.

Does any of this sound familiar? In Pagan circles it is unfortunately common to see people who have been subjected to "conversion therapy" and other abuses by families who felt that their sexuality or gender was "not what was best for them" or was "dangerous to society." Sorry to say, there are politicians active as of this writing who are reviving this old argument that it is society's job to forcibly police people's gender and sexuality. Let's take a moment to remember the dDraconian consequences this argument has had historically when it has been given the force of law.

Under the old system, people were also sometimes used as test subjects in clinical research without their knowledge or consent. These actions were deemed "appropriate" by doctors and governments at the time under the logic that the risk to these individuals was justified by benefits to the public good which would allegedly be born of the resulting discoveries about how to treat disease. An alarming number of people were fed or injected with diseases or radioactive substances in the 20th century without their knowledge or permission, in pursuit of "the greater good."

I want to discuss this attitude because I want to highlight how it may parallel the attitudes of other people in your life toward you. Too many people violate other people's autonomy, claiming to "just want what's best for them," or that their victim is being "selfish" by refusing to sacrifice their lives and their very selves for "the greater good." This argument may initially seem reasonable if it is coming from a parent or a partner who seems genuinely distressed, or a pastor or politician who claims that others are in genuine danger if you refuse to conform to their demands.

The medical atrocities of the 20th century show clearly the unacceptable nature of these demands. Would you insist that someone donate their bodies to science for dangerous experiments "for the greater good?" No? Then why would you ask someone to sacrifice their gender or sexuality, key parts of their personhood, based on the same argument?

Would you subject someone to medical incarceration or invasive medical procedures against their will "for their own good" because you did not believe they were competent to decide what is good for themselves? No? Then why would you try to force a change in their career or relationship based on the same belief?

In the international medical community today, best practices are built around patient autonomy. The idea is that doctors give recommendations about which courses of treatment will likely be best to achieve a patient's goals, but patients ultimately decide for themselves how they are treated. Patients have the right to decline treatment for any reason, to opt for more or less risky or invasive procedures as they see fit, and to choose which medications they take depending on their own experiences of side effects and concerns.

Per best practices for informed consent, for full patient autonomy these decisions should be considered, informed, and reversible. Patients should be informed of the benefits and risks of different treatments, given time to consider their options, and allowed to change their minds later if they wish without pressure from others or fear of negative repercussions from others.

This ideal is unfortunately not always the reality in modern medical treatment, where doctors too often fail to explain all of a patient's options, fail to fully explain the risks and benefits of treatments, or tell patients what they "must" do without exploring all options or taking a patient's personal goals into account. But the *ideal* of autonomy is one we can all benefit from meditating on.

What would it mean for all life decisions to be considered in this way? According to what you, as an individual, want out of life, rather than according to what some societal standard or authority figure tells you is "best?"

When helping patients make the best decisions for them, one of the first things doctors must do is determine what a patient's goals are for treatment. For many medical conditions, "living as long as possible" is a fairly universal goal, but some patients may prioritize quality of life over longevity, or the ability to engage in particular beloved activities over other abilities and outcomes.

Let's take a moment to think about what you prioritize, and what your goals are, and what choices you would make if not influenced by outside pressures.

Again, I encourage you to fantasize here and not allow yourself to be held back by preconceived notions about what is "realistic." To have any chance of

   1. Would you rather work from home, or commute to a work-

place outside your home?

2. Would you rather travel the world, or stay home?

3. Would you rather make as much money as possible quickly, or work as little as possible so you can spend your time doing other things?

4. What sorts of relationships would you like to experience, in your wildest fantasies? Who would they be with, and what would you do together?

5. What sort of community would you like to find or become part of? What would your ideal community look like?

6. What emotional experiences would you like to have each day, if you could choose?

7. What would you like to study, on your own or through a school, if you could study anything? Don't limit yourself to thinking about academic topics or programs which you know exist; I mean if you could study *anything*.

8. What sort of impact would you choose to make on the world, if you could spend your time doing anything?

We will use the answers to some of these questions later in the book. These are designed to give a glimpse into what a truly autonomous life would look like for you. While it is true that all beings are interdependent, and so we are somewhat constrained by our circumstances, it is likely that far more of the fantasies you have described above are possible than you may now believe.

To help you believe this, let me give you the example of myself. At the time I started my journey eight years ago by breaking the bonds that I knew were holding me back, I was working at a job which required me to spend most evenings and weekends at my local children's hospital and to sometimes be on-call. At the time in 2015, remote work was a rare privilege reserved for a precious few workers, and I was grateful to just have *any* job because the Great Recession had hit my home state harder than most in 2008. I was paying almost $400 per month in student debt on a $15 per hour salary. I had been told all my life that making a financial living as a writer—my true passion—was not feasible, and that only through working in science would I be able to create a future for myself.

At the time my interpersonal history was also, shall we say, not great. I had had several experiences of my closest friends disappearing on me, turning against me, or making more and more unreasonable demands of me until I snapped and cut them off entirely. I was in the midst of admitting that the healthier adult friendships I had not already cut off or been ghosted by were dysfunctional to the point that I could not rely on these friends to support me in the same ways I supported them.

I knew that I had a calling as a Pagan spiritual worker and culture-builder, but I couldn't seem to connect with even a single Pagan spiritual community in my hometown. One held meetings *only* during times I was required to be at work, and another shut down permanently almost as soon as I discovered they existed. At that time there were probably about half as many Pagans in the U.S. as there are today, and the Satanic Panic was not so far in the past; everyone around me generally considered it unreasonable to expect to really have a life doing Pagan work, and were skeptical that Pagan organizations and individuals doing real, serious work in the world even existed.

I do not *regret* this period of time. Being where I was taught me things I would not have learned in any other way; taught me useful ways of thinking I would not have learned. Being where I was allowed me to provide meaningful support in times and places where, otherwise, there would have been none.

The Pagan view of time and right and wrong is not one where there is one right way to do things and the other way is *wrong*; it is a view where things grow and change and cycle through seasons. Where living beings are processes, not static objects, and each stage of growth can be accomplished only by building upon the previous stage.

And there came a time where it became obvious that the life I had built was not sustainable. The principles I had been acting on for a decade were not going to get me to my goals. In fact, it became obvious that *no one* in my life was going to be able to reach their goals by continuing to do what we were doing then. I was not going to be able to write my books under the weight of my then-current responsibilities; my friends were not going to become free and independent by leaning on the little support I could give.

For growth to continue, a drastic change was needed. A Tower moment. A small Ragnarok, if you will.

Well... a year after my first Breaking of Bonds ritual, I was living in a different city, working in a different career which I had no degree in, and out of the relationships that had been giving me trouble. The work was far from over: it would be three years before I had financial security in my new career, and three years before I found the first Pagan community where I felt at home and found people who were seriously engaged in the kind of work I wanted to be doing. The learning curve was steep and painful.

It was also incredibly empowering. My power came, not from building up money in the bank or from people pleasing, but from being forced repeatedly to solve seemingly impossible problems until

I knew that I *could* solve almost any problem (and on short notice if I had to). I became more powerful, not by playing it safe, but by keeping my shit together *just* enough to continually grow my abilities and my knowledge.

Many who work with Loki find them to be a hard teacher. Tricksters are not famous for their gentle benevolence. They *are* famous for a certain kind of delight that comes from that wisdom which the ancients call "cunning." Tricksters are the sort to throw you into an impossible situation, and then when you find the solution you once believed did not exist, grin delightedly.

"See?" They'll ask you. *"That's what I wanted you to find."*

I must admit, this approach has worked better on me than any gentle encouragement.

Five years after I left my old life, I was safely battened down in Chicago when the pandemic hit. I soon found myself making more money than I ever had as the lockdowns removed a great many distractions and caused many business owners to turn toward long-term investments, including those I could provide with my writing services. As Pagan communities around North America went online for the first time to allow community meetings to continue in *some* fashion, I suddenly had access to teachers and communities hundreds and thousands of miles away who I never would have met otherwise.

Three years later I was a formal student of two Pagan organizations which were doing the sort of transformative work I had once dreamt of and been told was unrealistic. I spoke and danced at the Parliament of World Religions and sat in its Pagan Faith Room as a vibrant, global Pagan community blossomed all around me under the gaze of curious onlookers from other faiths. I began to publish my own books to widespread acclaim. I was now meeting people who were doing even *more* of what I wanted to be doing, creating even more of what I wanted to be creating, and whose lives and careers gave me a clear blueprint to keep working from.

Never say "impossible." Impossible, in my experience, is less a matter of the right elements being in place, and more a matter of whether you are willing to smack your head into the problem over and over again until it breaks.

Autonomy is not an *easy* road. It is frightening and painful. You may have heard of a little something called "rock bottom;" that place people usually have to reach before they admit the necessity to radically change their ways. It is arguable that I had a few "rock bottom" moments in the first few years of my journey—not in the sense that I had done something *wrong* or made *mistakes*, but in the sense that I realized, painfully, that I had to start doing things *differently* than I had before if I ever wanted to reach my goals.

But that's what the trickster's path is all about, isn't it? You're going to get scuffed up, get in trouble, get threatened by some eagles, get tied up under a snake.

But then you get out. And you get what you want. And what you want, probably, is a better, kinder world, created by the labor of people just like you smacking their heads against the walls of "what is possible" until they break.

So let's keep smacking, shall we?

Chapter Five

The Wisdom of the Body

Stop for a moment and listen to your body. Are you feeling a sense of freedom so far? Are you beginning to feel differently about what is possible for you, or feel parts of yourself you didn't know you had? You may even feel greater physical freedom of motion, looser limbs and deeper breaths. Your lungs may feel larger.

One of the most miraculous revelations I gained from studying with animist witches was how much magic lives in the body. We are talking about this now because your body will be an ally and a useful source of information as you do the work of autonomy. Even if your body has a great deal of pain, as with any companion of necessity, it is easier to work *with* it than *against* it, to take advantage of the resources that it *can* offer you on your journey.

I've met two witches and a healer in my life who I immediately knew I wanted to be like. I decided this because their mere presence changed everything about how I felt. Just being in their presence came with the most profound sense of safety. And where there is safety, I soon learned, things become possible that simply are not possible outside of the safe container. The activity of the entire nervous system changes. The body feels entirely different.

With my background in neuroscience, I can tell you that brain activity changes when this happens. Types of emotional processing and revelation are possible when the body feels safe and loved that are not possible when the nervous system thinks it is not safe to undertake a work of massive change.

I believe this is part of what witches mean when they say that they "stand between worlds." In almost all modern magic and witchcraft traditions, the preparation of a "container," often a witch's circle, is an important step. The traditional Wiccan incantation describes the state within a witch's circle as "perfect love and perfect trust."

Too often this is a mere platitude: if there is one thing I have learned, it is that exquisite care and some degree of firsthand experience is necessary to carry magic with you in the way these witches do; to make radical change possible by your very presence.

But it is possible. And the reason it is so powerful, the reason that it works, lies in the relationship between the body and the mind.

Join me in a couple of exercises to explore this relationship, if you will.

Exercise #1: The Glass Bubble

Close your eyes and envision all the threads that are pulling on you. In time, you may identify threads that pull you in the direction you *wish* to go, and you may design a bubble that permits only those desired bonds to remain intact. But, when you are first learning your true calling, there is the danger of confusing outside pressures with the calling from within. So, today, let's cut all the threads pulling on you from outside so that what is within can shine forth.

Take a few more deep breaths to center yourself in your body. Begin to imagine a glass bubble materializing around you, glowing gently with your energy.

As it solidifies, the bubble cuts every single thread of expectation or obligation that was pulling on you from outside yourself.

As the threads fall limp, you are free to sit up straighter, free of burdens or bonds.

See how you feel now. See what you *want* now that the bonds are cut. You may be surprised to feel like a completely new and much truer version of yourself.

You can stay in this state for as long as you like.

You can perform this exercise anytime, anywhere, as often as you like.

Some bonds you will surely choose to preserve, re-establish, and perhaps even strengthen. Let this exercise help you ensure that the bonds that guide you and hold you in place are of your free and conscious choosing, not imposed without your consent.

You can even examine individual bonds that you see pulling on your body when you perform this meditation. This can be an excellent way of discovering what in your life is exerting subconscious pressures on you. Such pressures often affect our bodies as well as our actions, and we can sometimes address problems with our actions by working within our bodies or vice versa.

What you learn from examining the bonds you find can help to highlight which choices you make to help you to feel better or worse. Paying attention to these sensations can help us to see where boundaries need to be set around activities or experiences that are holding you back, and where physical exercises such as yoga or dance may be useful.

Do you feel different now? In what ways does your body feel different? Did your posture change?

How might your entire body change if you spent more time in this state? One of the biggest surprises to me after I began my journey, and found that yoga was a key part of my spiritual growth, was how much my body changed. Things that I had always thought were "just the way my body was" proved to be connected to the state that I was living in.

We are not here to force change. But we are here to know that change is possible.

You can repeat this exercise as often as you like.

Exercise #2:

Be advised that this exercise may be triggering to those who cannot do body scans. While body scans are often recommended by therapists in a number of disciplines, some people with certain medical conditions or traumas can have overwhelming experiences if they try a traditional body scan.

This version is designed specifically to find any part of your body that feels *good*, but you can skip it if it starts to trigger you. If you are concerned about becoming overwhelmed, but you want to try and see what happens, you may wish to find a supportive person who can physically be with you and support you as you try it.

I was taught this exercise by a witch who was also a somatic therapist. She would hold free support group sessions in the back room of a metaphysical bookstore, in which she would slowly and gently teach people to address the stress in their body, to find the parts of their bodies and memories that felt good. This practice was called "resourcing," the process of finding the resources you already carry with you and leaning on them to help you feel secure and make change.

Is there any part of your body that feels good right now?

Is there any part of your skin that feels warm and safe and alive?

See if you can spread that feeling outward. See if you can study what it feels like and offer it to the body parts around it. Some parts of your body may hurt too much to absorb that feeling right now. But see how much of your body is able to feel good and safe in this moment.

Our emotions and our way of being live in the body. If we can find that part of the body which feels warm, which feels safe, which feels quiet, we do have some ability to move this feeling outward. When we identify the parts of our body that are feeling the way we want to feel, we can encourage other parts to learn to feel the same.

Feeling Consent in the Body

In the last couple of chapters, we have asked some questions to get an idea of what you do and don't want in your life. Years ago, I was privileged to work with the spiritual healer Emmanual Dagher, and he had an interesting and simple approach to determining whether a possibility was for or against what he calls your "highest good." Dagher does not identify as a witch, but he is a firm believer that the body is deeply in touch with the spirit's highest wisdom.

One of Dagher's discernment exercises centers on feeling for "expansion" and "contraction" in your body. These sensations often appear around the stomach or chest.

According to Dagher, a feeling of "expansion" in your body signals that an idea is probably in alignment with your highest good.

This makes sense both physically and metaphysically. If your body believes that something will help you to grow or expand your capabilities, responding by relaxing, allowing you to appear larger and stronger, and expanding your rib cage so you can take in more oxygen to undertake the task makes sense. This is also a logical response to something that will help you grow metaphysically, expanding the horizons of your experience and your wisdom and abilities.

A feeling of "contraction," on the other hand, signals an idea that is *not* in alignment with your highest good, according to Dagher. This, too, makes sense; an evolved response to that which is harmful often involves tensing and tightening muscles to prepare for a fight or flight response, and potentially slouching and curling up to try to hide. Metaphysically, things that are harmful result in a contraction of our possibilities, making us *less* able to live freely and walk in our power.

Try flipping back to your answers to the consent and boundaries questions about what you do and don't want in your life. As you review each item that you do or do not want, pay attention to your body.

Can you feel the sense of expansion and possibility that comes with the items you already know you would *like* to experience?

Can you feel a sense of contraction and fear from the items that you want to say "no" to?

Now try going back and reviewing your "yeses" again, breathing into the space of possibilities as you look forward to bringing these things into your life.

You may now wish to test your body's sensations of expansion and contraction on other decisions or situations you are facing.

The more sensitive you become to your body's innate sense of what is expansive for you and what is harmful to you, the more easily and decisively you will be able to say "no" to bad ideas and "yes" to good ones. You may even begin to notice that some things you *thought* you wanted begin to feel anxious and constricting as time goes on.

This is why we do this work. The body is not the enemy of the soul; they are its ally.

There are those theologians and psychologists who believe that disciplinarian approaches which teach that the body must be forced into submission by the mind are part of a concerted effort to rob individuals of power and authority, forcing them to rely on external authority figures for marching orders by severing their connection to their own internal senses of right and wrong.

Whether intentional or not, losing touch with the sensation of emotion in one's body is a common effect of trauma, and working with bodily sensations and the mind-body connection are considered important therapeutic modalities by many therapists who seek to help people step into their power.[1]

The Wisdom of the Body

Like most people raised in Western society, I was taught to view my body as a nuisance, a distraction, a source of weakness. "The flesh" was used as a shorthand by my Christian teachers to refer to that which tempts one to evil, that which is frail, that which is temporary. The very real attitude of many of my Christian elders was that the body is a sort of prison; this biological life is a test we are required to "pass" by exerting sufficient discipline to resist its temptations. Only once this life is over can we expect happiness or freedom.

This sentiment has traditionally been shared by the Western scientific community to a greater extent than many people realize. The science and science fiction authors I read growing up spoke almost exclusively of matters of the mind, stopping to address the body only

---

1. A., V. der K. B. (2015a). *The Body Keeps the Score: Brain, Mind, and Body in the Healing of Trauma*. Penguin Books.

when it hit an acute failure point which limited the mind. The body was viewed in many of these works as a troublesome chassis , and the ideal of achieving immortality and greater rationality and freedom by removing the mind from the body entirely was put forth in many works of futurism.

As of the 21st century, modern science is realizing the error of this view. Like a student moving along the Dunning-Kreuger curve, we are realizing the folly of fancying ourselves "rational"

In hindsight, the error is obvious: when we value the mind, it is the nervous system to which we are referring. And advancing science has shown more and more clearly that that nervous system, that part of the body which knows things and makes decisions, is not merely encased in a skull but woven throughout every part of our physical bodies.

It's clear why modern science came to the conclusions that it came to. The Christian attitude that the body and soul were completely separate entities, and that Pagan "superstitions" about the spiritual effects of various physical actions and beings were "irrational," probably didn't help. But many connections between the body and mind were also invisible to early scientific investigations.

A couple of centuries ago, Frankenstein was born when scientists began to figure out that electricity and certain chemicals could temporarily animate the muscles of a cadaver. For almost a century, that was about as far as the scientific knowledge of the mind-body went.

Chemicals, for example, can only be detected if you already know what you're testing for and have devised a way of rendering it visible to the eye. The nervous system speaks a language of chemicals, many of which I suspect remain undiscovered. We are still learning in leaps and bounds about the neurotransmitters and hormones that permeate our brains and guts and course through our blood. We know enough about these to know that we are still *missing* the existence of key actors.

One of the most promising avenues of 21st century research, in my opinion, is research into the chemicals found within the brain, the nerves, the air, the water, and the bacteria in our guts.

The earliest stages of this research have already detected what animist sages around the world described millennia ago, and what would have been lambasted as the most irrational of superstitions 50 years ago: an invisible communication network, through which humans, animals, plants and even weather systems communicate and influence each other.

In most cases, the specific chemicals being used to send messages have not yet been identified. But the results are there, piling up since these phenomena began to be studied seriously. We know that weather systems, soil bacteria, and the food we eat change our moods; that people can get a literal "whiff" of the emotions that have occupied a room in the recent or distant past, that being in the company of green things can speed the body's healing.

The utility of this information is obvious. We can learn things about the world by listening to senses that scientists long denied we even had. We can learn things about *ourselves* and our situations by feeling the sensations in our bodies; by feeling the sense of expansion that tells us a thing is good for us and the sense of contraction that tells us it may not be. We can create the experiences we want, create the *world* that we want, by understanding how the elements of the world speak to our bodies, and what is made possible or impossible by communion with our fellow living beings.

The magic I have experienced with the healers and witches I mentioned at the beginning of this chapter may have its roots in what is called "interpersonal limbic regulation"—the process by which people's nervous systems attune to each other.

We tend to view other people's mental states as trustworthy sources of information about the circumstances we are in, and our bodies will often change our own emotions and thoughts to match those of the people who are physically around us. This means that a person can invite profound change in the mental and emotional states of those around them by modulating their own mental and emotional states.

This is clearly not as easy as knowing that it's possible—most of us have not honed the skills to change our own mental and emotional states at will, let alone other people's. But it is one of many useful tools which has now been scientifically validated, and which can be used to change the world for better, or for worse.

We can hope that the day is coming when our instincts and our subtle perceptions will be treated as sources of useful information, not as failures of rationality. Indeed, more and more hospitals and schools are incorporating "mindfulness" practices to encourage people to make friends with their bodies and learn to listen to them.

A major reason for the increasing popularity of yoga is similar. Among yoga's numerous, surprisingly profound health benefits is a strengthening of nerve connections between the brain and body, leading to improved abilities to process and regulate one's emotions. Yoga is increasingly being offered or recommended by Western health facilities and acknowledged as a valid physical and mental health intervention.

But mainstream modern institutions are still a long way from the profound transformative abilities of the witches I have known who can skillfully create containers where the changing of the world can begin. It is my hope that the study of these arts will continue, both in the laboratory and in the community.

Chapter Six

Invalidating Environments in Biosocial Theory

I n the course of my research for this book, I ran across an idea that helped make sense of many things I've observed as a friend and a community healer. In the course of my work, I've often encountered people who were clearly in profound distress—but who struggled to justify to themselves *why*, because their families or environments didn't seem "as bad" as the circumstances of some other people they knew.

In researching this matter, I stumbled across the concept of an "invalidating environment" in Dialectical Behavioral Therapy. I want to share my findings here, because I believe some of the DIY techniques of DBT hold tremendous promise for helping both ourselves and others to become more comfortable with our own emotions and desires, and to step into our power. DBT also provides a powerful framework for explaining why we sometimes feel so angry or distressed in certain social situations, even if they are not obviously abusive.

As a disclaimer, I am not a therapist. I have found the legal and clinical parameters of psychotherapy a little bit limiting to the work I do, especially since politicians in various states can impose legal requirements on how licensed therapists must behave toward their clients without necessarily having any scientific backing for these decisions.

There is also the matter of accessibility which we desperately need to be discussing as a society. As of this writing, a psychotherapeutic master's degree at a can routinely cost about $100,000 for three years of study, even if the program was taken remotely. When we combine this with the requirement in most states for a new therapist to perform *3,000 hours* of unpaid labor as supervised interns, we have a real, serious problem on the matter of who is financially able to become a licensed therapist, and how these therapists are allowed to serve our communities.

All that being said, I am *deeply* supportive of psychotherapeutic methods that are backed by clinical evidence of their effectiveness, and I will recommend psychotherapy methods which are backed up by clinical evidence over religiously-based mental health counseling any day of the week.

Religious texts, after all, are open to be interpreted vastly differently by different counselors, and are not written based on safety and effectiveness data. One of the more horrifying discoveries I made while researching programs in pastoral counseling was that some religious organizations offer "crisis counseling programs" which appear to include *no clinical science-based training whatsoever* and are exclusively based in some religious leader's interpretation of scripture.

One of the psychotherapeutic methods that *is* based on clinical evidence of its effectiveness is Dialectical Behavioral Therapy. Often called "DBT" for short, this therapy is based on the assumption that behavior stems from a "dialectic"—a fancy word stemming from the same root as "dialogue"—between a person and their environment. By becoming aware of this interplay and learning to breathe in the space between environment and response, a person can take control of their actions and to some extent their emotions.

In clinical studies, DBT has been one of the most effective methods at improving the quality of life of people with Borderline Personality Disorder. More recent explorations have found that it shows promise for treating many other kinds of emotional distress and self-destructive behavior.

One of the major theories discussed in DBT is Biosocial Theory, in which behavior results from the dialectic (or dialogue) between a person's biology, their body, and their social environment.[1]

On the face of it, this explanation for behavior makes a tremendous amount of sense. We have seen in the previous chapter how emotion arises in our bodies. In this book so far we have focused on bodily emotions that give us useful information about what feels *good*, but fear, shame, and rage are also emotions of the body. The idea that these emotions interact with our environment, particularly with the way others *respond* to our emotions, to create our behavior, makes a huge amount of sense.

This explanation leaves room to discuss both personal emotions and environmental factors, including the impact of genetic predispositions and cultural factors on mental illness and behavior. In this

---

1. Staff, B. (2021, October 28). *What the heck is the biosocial theory?*. Behavioral Psych Studio. https://behavioralpsychstudio.com/what-the-heck-is-the-biosocial-theory/

model, a person's genetic makeup interacts with a person's circumstances and prevailing culture, and the task of therapy is to help both the person and the environment become more supportive toward the outcomes we want to see.

It turns out that the practical recommendations of DBT have a lot in common with what we have covered so far: in order to gain comfort in handling one's emotions and reactions, a person must become friends with their body, learn how emotions originate in the body, and learn to disrupt uncontrollable emotional responses in the body using exercises that change the neurological state of the body directly. One must also learn to "validate" one's own emotions, confirming for oneself that one's likes, dislikes, intuition, feelings of hurt or joy, etc., are valid sources of information and valid ways of being.

DBT originator Dr. Marsha Linehan believes that pathological behaviors generally come from extreme, and sometimes unstable, reactions to mismatches between a person's bodily emotions and their environment.

The thought is this: we tend to internalize the things our caregivers tell us during childhood, and tell ourselves these same things as adults. If a person is often told that their emotions are irrelevant, bad, or wrong, this can lead to problems in a number of aways.

A person may react by ignoring or denying their own emotions, which can lead to uncontrollable outbursts of behavior when enough emotion builds up in the body and breaks free of conscious control. A person may react by becoming aggressively combative about their feelings, expecting based on past experience that others will be invalidating and unsupportive, regardless of whether the other person is actually supportive or not. A person may swing wildly between invalidating their own emotions, experiencing crippling self-doubt and people-pleasing behavior, and combatively defending their emotions by lashing out at people around them.

There is a growing body of evidence that more common forms of mental distress including anxiety, depression, and non-suicidal self-harm may also be positively correlating to what DBT calls "invalidating environments;" environments where people are made to feel, for any number of reasons and in any number of ways, that their emotions are bad, wrong, or invalid.

The interesting thing is that this explanation dovetails well with what I have observed in my coaching clients. People often come to me expressing that they cannot understand why they feel so distressed, or become so uncontrollably angry with certain people in their lives, even though these people don't seem to be behaving overtly abusively. Some profess that they feel there must be something wrong with *them* since they feel unhappy and inadequate, even though they had an upbringing that *appeared* prosperous, peaceful, and supportive compared to what many of their friends endured.

Many people express wondering how someone else can "make them crazy" so effectively even when nothing seems obviously wrong on the outside. This principle is a huge part of why one of the first steps I recommend for people looking to break unhealthy cycles is to move out of distressing living situations as fast as they possibly can. It simply does not seem possible to live with people who treat us in certain ways and retain our sanity, even if these people are not violently abusive or neglectful in obvious ways.

And there is one word that describes the type of behaviors these people have experienced: invalidating. Whether it's relationships that are overtly abusive, perfectionistic families who put incredible pressure on their children to live up to ideals, or seemingly ordinary families who insist on projecting their own emotions onto their children, a similar creeping feeling of lack of adequacy and self-worth seem to be common.

For one specific, humorous example, I once guiltily recounted to my therapist that I had screamed at someone for offering me a sandwich. Why? Because they had offered me a sandwich *no less than 21 times* in 20 minutes, disregarding my answer of "no" each time I gave it and repeating the question a minute later.

This person couldn't believe that I genuinely didn't want a sandwich because *they* felt that I *should* want a sandwich, and they trusted their own assessment of my emotions more than they trusted what I was explicitly telling them about my emotions. And I was the one left feeling "crazy," because who screams at someone for trying to give them a sandwich?

That's an excellent, if extreme, example of benign-seeming invalidation.

According to Linehan's theory of DBT, there are four common classes of behaviors which can be invalidating. These include:

- Communications of inaccuracy. This is the principle operating in the sandwich example: the idea that you are wrong about your own emotions, wrong about what you want, or that your feelings and ideas are inherently wrong and need to be "corrected." This creates a deep distrust in one's own judgment, and can produce a sense that one is inadequate or even a burden if one's true feelings are treated as intrusions on community life when they are expressed.

- Misattribution. In misattribution, one person tells another that they are wrong about their own feelings or motives, often attributing the person's true feelings to malice or weakness. This is what happens when someone accuses you of being manipulative when you express your true feelings, or tells you that you only feel that way because you are weak, lazy, selfish, etc..

- Discouraging negative emotional expression. This is related to what has become known in pop psychology recently as "toxic positivity," where negative emotions are treated as harmful and discouraged. This is in some ways the saddest form of invalidation, because it often comes from people whose primary goal is genuinely to help you, but the only way they know to do that is to "make the pain go away" by behaving as though it is not real. I would strongly recommend that folks who engage in this behavior read the "Six Levels of Validation" worksheet linked later in this chapter, as this worksheet gives an extremely powerful and easily reproducible method to help someone who is hurting in an empowering way instead of an invalidating one.

- Oversimplification of problem solving. In this invalidation technique, a person insists that it is "simple" or "easy" to solve a problem or cope with a situation, thereby invalidating feelings of distress around a situation. This can include the classic "you're overreacting" or "a normal person wouldn't be upset by this," as well as the "why don't you just do _____?" that people who express distress are too often met with.

Together, behaviors like these work to create a situation where people do not trust their own emotions and are afraid to express them for fear of being deemed bad, wrong, or unacceptable. People who have consistently encountered invalidating behavior may hesitate to make decisions or take action because they don't trust their own judgment. They may even lose the ability to *feel* their emotions, to identify what their bodies are doing because they have been taught that reacting truthfully to the emotions in their bodies is wrong and dangerous.

This picture of invalidating behavior allows us to account for behavior by chaotic families, "perfect" families, and typical families. It also hints at cultural origins for some types of self-destructive behavior: in cultures which routinely prescribe that people be told their thoughts and emotions are bad and wrong, and that they be "molded" into having the "correct" thoughts and emotions, it might not be surprising that certain types of emotional distress and self-destructive behavior become endemic.[2]

So how does one improve this situation? And, just as importantly for our purposes, why *should* one seek to improve it? Do we learn to work with our emotions in order to meet some external standards of acceptability, or in order to accomplish what we want to accomplish in life?

Toward the end of this chapter, we will discuss a few common criticisms of DBT whose answers I believe are useful to keep in mind as we consider using these ideas and tools in our own lives. There is one common point of confusion that I want to address now, though, *before* we sample some exercises based in the philosophy of DBT. This

---

2. Musser, N., Zalewski, M., Stepp, S., & Lewis, J. (2018). A systematic review of negative parenting practices predicting borderline personality disorder: Are we measuring biosocial theory's 'invalidating environment'? *Clinical Psychology Review, 65,* 1–16. https://doi.org/10.1016/j.cpr.2018.06.003

is the difference between "invalidation of one's feelings" and "criticism of one's behavior."

Many people object that validating a person's feelings must, necessarily, be the same thing as condoning their behavior. It's easy to see how someone might reach this conclusion: actions are a response to feelings, so people who are not intimately familiar with the space in which we can *choose* our responses to feelings might feel that actions and feelings are essentially the same thing.

However, the entire philosophy of DBT is that we *can* use methods to *modify* our behavioral responses to our feelings—and that denying that our feelings exist actually makes our responses to them *more* unmanageable. We can only influence and manage that which we acknowledge and pay attention to. After all, if we insist something simply is not happening, or that the happening is intolerably evil, we are unlikely to be able to respond to it in a thoughtful and wise way.

If we cannot acknowledge our emotions and hold them tenderly, we are instead *more* likely to completely lose control of our internal situation.

It is my belief that this is why so many moralistic teachers are found to be committing serious abuses by the end of their careers. If they refuse to accept or validate emotions they see as "unacceptable" in themselves, their impulse control is likely to suffer tremendously. Their thinking may become twisted to attribute motives they see as morally acceptable for their uncontrolled behaviors, which is one of the more dangerous phenomena that can happen in human behavior.

So when we speak of validating emotions, we do not mean that we accept abusive or harmful behaviors from ourselves or others. We mean that, by accepting, validating, and becoming friends with these emotions, we gain the ability to choose our responses to them more thoughtfully and freely.

One core tenant of Emmanuel Dagher's Core Work healing method is the idea that all emotions have *some* sort of helpful basis. Even the most violent anger is, at some level, intended to protect someone. The question is, is this emotion serving its intended purposes with the way we are responding to it now? When we befriend even our most socially unacceptable emotions, we can ask what these emotions are *really* trying to accomplish, and whether our reactions to those emotions are helping us to be who we want to be and do what we want to do.

Without further ado, let's explore a few exercises you can do at home to support yourself and others in the face of the strong emotions that are likely to come with making change.

Regulating the Nervous System

Since DBT teaches that emotion is a biological response which comes through the body, some suggested coping mechanisms involve using sensations and movement to soften the body's response during moments of overwhelming emotion. Emily Daily of the Dialectical Behavioral Therapy Center suggests using one or more of the "six senses" to help the body regulate its nervous system activity during overwhelming moments. These senses include:

- Sight: Looking at something that inspires positive emotion, such as a photograph, a cute or funny video, or a beautiful natural vista, as a way of softening overwhelming emotion.

- Touch: Touching or playing with something textured or fun, like a fidget spinner or silly putty, petting an animal, giving someone a hug, or taking a bath or shower to regulate nervous system activity.

- Smell: Using aromatherapy such as from candles, lotions, or a favorite food to create feelings of pleasure and relaxation to soften an overwhelming emotion.

- Taste: Mindfully eating a favorite drink or beverage that you enjoy to focus the nervous system.

- Sound: Listen to a favorite song, or real or recorded nature sounds, to calm the nervous system.

- Movement: Getting up and walking, dancing, or exercising can help.[3]

The idea behind all of these techniques is that, since emotion occurs in the nervous system, overwhelming emotion can be softened by introducing new physical stimuli that will change the activity of some parts of the nervous system. For many this can soften the impact of overwhelming emotions to allow a person to process these emotions over time instead of all at once, which allows for more understanding and a more thoughtful response to occur.

Acceptance of Pain

One key to the DBT perspective is that accepting pain makes pain easier to deal with, while fighting against pain or trying to avoid it actually makes it worse.

---

3. Daily, E. (2022, July 28). *3 skills for responding to invalidating environments.* Behavioral Psych Studio. https://behavioralpsychstudio.com/3-skills-for-responding-to-invalidating-environments/

Many commentators from different disciplines have commented on this over the years. Buddhist philosopher Alan Watts and Mark Manson, author of "The Subtle Art of Not Giving a F*ck" are among those who have registered the opinion that: "Wanting a positive experience is a negative experience; accepting a negative experience is a positive experience."[4]

This may be one of the reasons why validation of one's pain—acceptance that it is real, and it is difficult, and it is *important*—yields superior results to the toxic positivity MO of insisting that "it's not that bad," or that it's not "correct" to feel pain over what has happened. Denial of pain prevents it from being processed and accepted; acceptance allows it to be processed, completed, learned from.

Where I differ from the Buddhists here is that I don't believe that *negative* experiences are always *bad*. Reframing pain as an opportunity to exercise acceptance doesn't make things better; hitting rock bottom does. Very often, radical change for the better can only occur when the pain of the current situation has become intolerable.

And, very often, a situation does not actually have to become physically worse to spark radical change. But the pain the situation is causing has to be validated, acknowledged, and accepted instead of continuing to be invalidated and denied.

So the lesson here is not "it's our job to accept infinite pain without complaint;" it's that, when pain does occur, accepting it and looking for how, if at all, it may have benefitted us allows us to move *through* the pain in wisdom and strength, instead of becoming overwhelmed by resentment of the past and fear of the future.

---

4. Manson, M. (2019). *The subtle art of not giving a f*ck: A counterintuitive approach to living a good life*. HarperLuxe.

The Six Levels of Validation

The Center for Dialectical Behavioral Therapy also links to a hand-out summarizing Linehan's Six Levels of Validation, which I believe may be one of the more useful tools for teaching people to support each other that I have ever encountered. You will find a link to this handout in the footnote at the bottom of this page. I highly encourage you to use this link, and share it.

Unfortunately, in full transparency, I am having trouble attributing this handout properly to its maker. It is linked to by the DBT Center, hosted by the website of the Minnesota state government, and has no author or institutional name on it. It clearly makes use of Dr. Linehan's work, but there is no obvious indication as to whether these are her precise words or whether her ideas have been distilled by somebody else who deserves credit here.

If anybody knows precisely who created this handout so that I can credit them, please do reach out to me at my email address located in the front and back matter of this book. In the meantime, use the link at the bottom of this page to access and share the handout if you wish. I will recap its contents with my own unique spin based on my own experiences below:[5]

1. Level One: Stay awake and pay attention. Attention has transformative power. It is my firm belief that part of the

---

5. Six levels of Validation Level One: Stay awake and pay attention. https://www.co.grant.mn.us/DocumentCenter/View/2701/Levels-of-Validation-Handout

profoundly healing magic of the witches I mentioned in Chapter 5 was their ability to see a person with complete, undivided, loving attention. These expert-level witches did not need to use any words to communicate that they are seeing and loving you; they had sufficient command of their own nervous systems that their body language, their facial expressions, the sensation of their focused presence was sufficient. But for those of us who are less expert, asking questions like "can you tell me more?" can help to demonstrate that we are actively paying attention.When you are sitting with someone and trying to help them, try devoting your entire being to looking at them and seeing them for who they are during the work. Try turning this same loving attention on yourself, the way you would do for another person. Try finding other people who will do this for you in turn.

2. Level Two: Accurate Reflection. Show the person that you hear what they are saying by repeating their words back to them. Whether this should be literal repetition of the person's words or your own attempt to paraphrase what they are saying depends on which practitioner you ask. Either way, there is something about having another person voice your own feelings that makes those feelings real, valid, important. And powerful.Of note, accurately reflecting someone's feelings back to them does *not* mean agreeing with those feelings, or with the thoughts and ideas the person has attached to them.This is an important note because we can help someone to heal—including healing their behaviors—by validating their feelings. We don't have to agree with their beliefs and ideas in order to validate their emotions, and they don't

get to insist that we must agree with their beliefs and ideas or we are invalidating their feelings. Validating someone's emotions and agreeing with their beliefs are two different things. Beliefs are a *response* to a feeling, and we have the ability to *choose* different responses to the same emotions. A great deal of harm can come from insisting that there is only one possible response to a given emotion, or that it is unsupportive and invalidating to disagree with someone's beliefs.

3. Level Three: Say What Hasn't Been Said. This is delicate territory, because what we really want to *avoid* is making *incorrect* statements about what someone feels; having them feel obligated to agree with us even though those statements don't accurately match their emotions. But when done properly, this can help people to voice and acknowledge emotions that they may have struggled to articulate, or may have been too afraid to voice. You can try asking questions like "Do you think that you feel _____?" or "I wonder if you feel _____?" In addition to potentially helping a person articulate what they have been afraid of or unable to say, showing that another person has taken the time to think about their emotions and wants to know more about them has its own therapeutic value.

4. Validating Using History or Biology. One reason I like to discuss the science behind our perceptions in my books is that it can be incredibly validating to learn that there is objective, scientific support for your experiences. I think it's a bad idea to try to use science to determine what someone "should" be feeling or perceiving. As we discussed in Chap-

ter 5, doing science isn't *easy*, and there are a great many mechanisms and principles which modern science probably hasn't figured out yet. Modern science may, in fact, need to learn what to study from our experiences, which is all the more reason to validate and explore these experiences. But confirming that someone's perceptions or emotions *make objective sense* using biology goes a long way toward helping a person to trust their bodies and their instincts. Another recommended method is using a person's personal history to validate that their emotions make sense ("it makes sense for you to feel that way since this has happened in your past").

Of note, once again, validating that someone's emotions make sense *based on their personal history* is not the same as suggesting that their beliefs or responses are inescapable or objectively correct. To use an example from the linked handout, saying "It makes sense that you'd feel uncomfortable since your boss looks like your ex-husband" is not the same as saying "it is true that all men who look like your ex-husband will hurt you." But validating that the emotion is real and *makes sense* is often necessary *before* one can explore whether a response to that emotion of treating one's boss as the enemy or being afraid of being hurt at work is serving one's goals.

1. Normalizing. After showing that a person's emotions make sense given their personal history or biology, a next step can be to point out that anyone in their situation would likely feel the same way. Their feeling, then, is not aberrant or "wrong"—it's a logical and valid conclusion stemming from their personal history.Another technique I like to use some-

times is the use of *world* history to notify people if I am aware of some great person of history, or some culture, which had similar feelings or practices to the person's own conclusions. The idea that "this isn't just me, it's an actual thing that other people have historically acknowledged" can also help. This is a good time to reinforce why validating a person's emotions is particularly powerful *as a way of separating emotions from actions.* The holy grail of DBT is the space in which a person is able to freely and thoughtfully *choose* how to respond to their emotions. This actually becomes *easier* when a person understands that it is not their *feelings* that are being attacked when their *actions* are criticized or met with boundaries. The realization that a person can choose how to respond to their feelings, that there is not just one possible valid behavioral response, is key to giving people the power to take actions that benefit their goals. And re-evaluating whether one's actions are in alignment with one's goals is easier when one understands that one's *emotions* make sense and are even supported by others, but that there are multiple responses a person can choose to those emotions.

2. Radical genuineness. This process of validation is ultimately a process of communication. It's not just about validating how another person feels: there is also a time to help them see how other people feel, and take that into consideration when they are choosing their future responses to their emotions. This is a time to be honest with a person about your feelings toward them, and their impact on you. Very often, if we are taking the time and energy to do this work, it is because the person is genuinely important to us in some way.

That does not mean that their actions can't be hurtful to us, and it would be unhelpful to pretend that it does. But that, again, is a core part of this work: you are important to me, *and* this action you took hurt me. This thing you said hurt me *because* you are important to me, and I like to believe that you feel well of me. You are important to me, and *that's why* I hope you can find a different response to this self-destructive behavior, because I don't think it's going to help you get to where you want to be in life.In this way, we can enforce that the person is seen and valued, and that their emotions are valid and real and important. And we do this in a way that divorces the actions we are concerned about from their humanity and their emotions.

When you are ready, I would encourage you to find a group or partner to use these steps with. It is a good idea to prepare for seismic emotional shifts to occur: this level of being seen and valued is enough to bring most people to tears very quickly.

It is a good idea to have a support plan for what to do if someone becomes overwhelmed and has an uncontrollable reaction. Just like with magic and with medication, all powerful work has the potential for powerful, unexpected side effects.

But that is why we undertake this work: because it is powerful. And at the end of the day, we are here to make change.

Avoiding Excess With DBT Methodologies

Before we close this chapter, I want to discuss a few common criticisms of DBT methodology. I want to discuss them because they all have a point. I think it's important to acknowledge both the risks of relying blindly on this framework, and the benefits which, in my opinion, make the tools discussed here useful when used wisely with an understanding of the imperfections of the DBT framework.One criticism from DBT from the clinical community has been that there are no generally accepted measurements to measure invalidation. The definition of "invalidating behavior" covers a wide variety of relationship dynamics, which has led some to argue that it is too vague. I personally find the explanatory power of the DBT framework, and the clinical results it gets, to be sufficiently compelling that I don't see this vagueness as a weak point.

Another criticism of DBT is the claim that validating unwanted emotions encourages them, and may act to *discourage* self-discipline. While we can see how a person could reach that conclusion using pure, abstract logic, this is why clinical research is needed to determine what is really the best way to move forward as a society. Because in practice, what we see is that unwanted emotions do not simply disappear. Our physical reactions don't disappear; they only become buried and built up in our bodies, eventually coming out in uncontrollable ways.

What we see when we look at clinical studies is that, in practice, validating emotions *helps* to regulate them. When emotions are denied and invalidated, they are often not allowed to process out through the body, and the shame and fear that is created can actually make a person's emotional reactions *more* uncontrollable in the future. When emotions are validated, accepted, received, and processed, however, *then* it becomes possible to take what is useful from them and teach the mind and body new ways of reacting.

In a very real way, we can *only* regulate our emotions successfully when we are not in denial about them. And part of my core thesis is that we are most powerful when we regulate our emotions in accordance with our *own* goals and visions of what we wish to achieve, not when we are *told* how to feel by outside forces who are powerful, and therefore inherently potentially corrupt.

The last common criticism of DBT is more relevant to our goals. Taken to an extreme, the methods and philosophy of DBT can be used to convince a person who is being mistreated that their emotional reaction to their mistreatment is extreme or unmanageable, and that it is their job to use DBT methods to accept and cope with their sub-standard situation. DBT practitioners have sometimes been criticized for counseling that leaving a situation or relationship be a last resort, and that patients focus on managing their own emotional responses.

I am a big fan of the idea of using useful tools to your own ends. I believe we can probably all agree that the tools of DBT are *useful* for helping ourselves and others. You have probably felt the empowering and soothing effects of these techniques already in the course of reading this chapter.

If something is useful, use it. But be mindful of what you are using it *for*: we who are undertaking this work of breaking our bonds are probably not doing so just so we can tolerate our situations more effectively. We are doing so because we want to create *better* situations, more in alignment with our truest callings.

We wish to become more comfortable with our own emotions and their management, not so that we can remain submissive and meek, but so that we can tolerate the risks and changes we may need to take on in order to get to where we want to be. We may also wish to become more peaceful people who can respond to others with more nurturing and equanimity; indeed, I believe most of us have that goal.

But this, too, is not the same thing as "tolerating bullshit." The ideal is to cultivate the ability to *both* be calm and nurturing *or* firm and confrontational, depending on what *we* feel the situation calls for. It is in this way that people are empowered to make change as they see fit.

Step Into Your Power

When you do the exercise of validating yourself and others, you will find that a sense of power begins to build. That is why I have made this the last chapter in the "To Know" portion of this book. I believe that we have now done sufficient exploratory work regarding who we are, how we feel, and what we want—questions we are too rarely asked in earnest—to begin formulating our will.

I want to leave you with a few simple exercises to do with another person or a group which will illustrate, physically and in your body, the power you are capable of. These exercises are less in-depth than the full six levels of validation, and are more targeted to explore the empowerment that comes from validation.

With your partner or your group, I invite you to take turns discussing the following questions. As you discuss each question, allow time to notice how your body is feeling as you talk, and as other people respond to you. Notice the changes in your body and allow yourself to fully perceive these. As often as you like, pause and pay attention to these changes in your body, to form a memory of what they feel like.

1. What was something that happened to you as a child that you felt you were never allowed to talk about? What happened, and how did it make you feel? How might your life have been different if the people around you had taken you seriously then, and taken action around what happened?

2. What was a time when you were right and someone in authority was wrong? Why do you think you were able to see

the truth more clearly than they could? How might things have been different if they had listened to you in time and made changes accordingly?

3. What do you still feel that you shouldn't talk about? What emotion or experience do you have that you feel or fear is invalid, or that you believe no one wants to hear about? What would happen if you not only trusted your emotion or experience, but took action based upon it to try to make things better for the people who come after you?

Sit with your reactions to these questions for as long as you like.

Chapter Seven

True Will

We have spent most of this book so far on getting to know ourselves. This is important, because people in substandard situations often learn to ignore themselves. When there is never room for your thoughts, feelings, or ambitions, you can become physically numb to what those are. We are taught from almost every corner of society not to say "no," not to have needs, not to listen to our bodies.

This can result in putting your magical efforts toward things that it turns out you don't actually *want*, because they are what you think you *should* want, or what you thought you wanted long ago. You're not going to get what you want if you put your effort into working toward something that you *don't* actually want. This is why we have spent a full five chapters on progressing further and further towards listening to our bodies and making room to listen to the Will that bubbles up out of us.

Once we have accomplished the step of "To Know," the next step in the Witch's Pyramid is "To Will." If To Know is associated with the East, the direction of the sunrise, of air, and of conflict which reveals the truth, To Will is associated with the South. The direction of Fire.

In tarot, the suit of Wands is associated with Fire. Wands are sometimes pictured as the tool used by magicians to inscribe their Will upon the world; they are sometimes pictured as kindling, fuel to power a consuming blaze. Fire is explored in all its aspects, from the steady hearthfire that warms the cozy family home to the consuming blaze which destroys the old growth that chokes new life.

When Pagans and occultists speak of Will, they do not only mean one's wishes for this particular moment. They are referring to the deep-seated drive and mission which wells up out of Divine spark which is the human soul, to the role of the individual as a co-creator of reality. Let's take a moment to examine a few different ways of sensing and thinking about one's Divine spark.

True Will in Occult Traditions

A number of Pagan and occult traditions speak of enacting one's Will as being the goal of magic, framing the goal of worship not as complete submission of a sinful human to some authoritative God, but as a communion which recognizes that you are *part* of God. The goal here is not to extinguish oneself and be subsumed by some superior being; it is to ignite oneself into fulfilling the mission you were put into the world to accomplish.

Statements such as "Do What Thou Wilt Shall Be the Whole of the Law" have often been criticized by imperial religions as a selfish and immoral mindset; simply "getting what you want" out of life, they argue, is a destructive and short-sighted moral code (and admittedly Crowley's formulation contains no caveats about also protecting the free will of other beings).

I disagree with the thesis that individual will is generally selfish and destructive. In fact, I think we can learn a good deal about what human Will is like by looking at what oppressive governments feel the need to outlaw, and what they need to force people to do.

The sorts of religious and political movements that argue that prioritizing the actualization of one's own Will is selfish, what do they generally forbid people from doing?

They forbid people from loving. They try to force all manner of human relationships into narrowly defined nuclear family units, painting love outside of these boundaries as an evil and destructive force. They forbid people from compassion, using the cry that it is evil to tolerate "sin" to try to shame people into silence as "sinners" are violently punished. They forbid people from healing. They forbid almost all spiritual arts which have historically been used to heal trauma and physical illness, and to empower people. They forbid people from defending themselves from predation and oppression. They tell people to say "yes" to authority figures no matter what, and often ban ideas which may lead women, children, and peasants to question the supremacy of the ruling class or arm them with tools to resist their demands.

And what do they mandate? They mandate obedience, first and foremost. When their gods and leaders commit atrocities, we are told to forgive and forget human failings; when we commit the smallest act of disobedience, the smallest act of unapproved love or compassion, we are told that we are wicked and must rely on these authority figures for our discernment and our marching orders. Often, they mandate violence. Wars that these leaders choose to undertake are "holy," and it is an abdication of moral duty to refuse to kill other human beings in their service. Destruction of the natural world is "progress," and engaging in spiritual relationships with our plant and animal kin, with the Earth and the sky, is "idolatrous." Women and children who refuse to tolerate abuse are "ungrateful" and "rebellious," while authority figures who violently punish nonviolent "sins" "just want what's best for you" and are doing you a service by "instilling discipline.

This is why we turn to witchcraft.

From the first days of the Neopagan Renaissance, this has been very explicit. Aradia appears specifically to women and peasants, to teach them to defend themselves from those who would like to treat them violently with no consequences. Papa Gede and Papa Legba, who you met in Chapter 1, hail from the same traditions that produced the most successful revolution in the world ever to be staged by enslaved people. The rise of pantheistic magical traditions which teach that individuals have their own divine moral authority has been accompanied by decreases in war and violence around the world.

So maybe individual Will isn't so bad, after all.

In the occult traditions which celebrate Will, "Will" with a capital "W" has a specific meaning. It refers not to the whim of the moment, but to the soul's deepest desire and mission in life. In magical traditions, human souls are often thought of as literal sparks of the Divine, with each of us intended to be co-creators with the other Divine powers. A person's True Will is what the Divine spark of the soul intends to create in the world.

A way to think about one's mission in life that may be wiser, because it relies less on intellectual rationalizing and more on sensing the feelings in one's body, is the concept of "following one's bliss."

Follow Your Bliss

Author Joseph Campbell, who wrote extensively about comparative religion, what we now call "the hero's journey," and of accumulating power and wisdom, advised his students simply to "follow their bliss."

This is as simple as it sounds: pursue what makes you feel blissful.

I have to say, I can endorse this simple prescription. Much of what I am doing now was *not* consciously planned in the early days of my magic, because, to be quite frank, I would not have thought it was even *possible* for me to be where I am today eight years ago.

I had just about accepted that perhaps I could become a successful writer; the idea that I could become a successful Pagan healer, part of a community of *thousands* of people who understand and appreciate and share my relationship with my patron god, and be getting taken somewhat seriously by teachers of other world religions, well...I just would not have been able to see any possible mechanism for that to happen.

Perhaps more significantly, none of the mechanisms I *could* see felt right. There were technically Pagan initiatory traditions available to me—but none of them felt right. There were interfaith seminaries which *also* did not feel right. And in hindsight, that is probably a good thing, because if I had gone by any of those routes I probably would not have met the people I *did* meet by following my bliss: the people who walk off the beaten path, and who, like me, were called to create new paths that did not even exist to be factored into my plans eight years ago.

So, I didn't ask for where I am today, in my early magic. I asked for something different. Which I got and realized I was unsatisfied with within a few years. But all along the way, I kept "following my bliss"—even as I traveled North America following the annual circuit of writers' conferences, it was the Pagan gatherings I attended in each city I visited that I couldn't keep myself away from. And attending them, eventually, created new paths that had not existed before.

There is one more way of conceptualizing one's Will or mission in life that I would like to discuss here, because I find it to be a useful framework.

The Soul Contract

Some spiritual traditions refer to a concept of "soul contracts," which in my opinion is also a useful concept here. The idea of a "soul contract" is that souls are able to choose where and when they incarnate, and that they have incarnated in a particular time and place for a particular reason. The soul's "contract" with the world is that they will undertake certain experiences for specific reasons, with the intention of accomplishing a certain mission while they're there.

The idea of the "soul contract" has been criticized by some as a form of "toxic positivity" which trivializes suffering, but I believe there is a reason why healers from a number of different traditions have found this idea useful in their work. At the Parliament of World Religions this year, I had the privilege of listening to Reverend Doctor Joanne Coleman speak on her method for helping people heal from trauma.

Coleman is a fascinating woman who drew on expertise ranging from the original Aramaic versions of certain Christian prayers to Gullah Geechee folk magic in describing her approach to bringing love and kindness into the world.

"I tell people, 'whatever happened to you, it cannot touch your Divinity.'" She leaned forward and looked into our eyes as she said it, saying it *to* us rather than merely as a recitation. "Nothing that happens to you can touch your Divinity."

Then she followed up with a question that she herself prefaced with, "Now, I'm going to ask you a very rude question. What good came from it?"

The trend in some circles currently is to argue that speculating about *good* that may have come from hardship and trauma is oppressive because it may be used to argue that hardship and trauma are justified. Rev. Dr. Coleman felt differently. By looking for the good that can be gleaned from even the most awful of events, she felt that her charges were regaining a sense of agency and control over their lives. Their trauma was no longer something that happened *to* them; it was something that, in some small way, happened *with* them, something that in some small way they could turn to their benefit and power.

Whether or not one is inclined to believe in the idea that one's soul literally chose to inhabit this particular body in this particular time and place, the attitude of finding strengths and advantages in even the most unlikely of places probably boosts a person's chance of success in accomplishing what they *know* they want to accomplish in life. When we cannot go through established channels of power to accomplish what needs to be done, what is left is finding every advantage in every place that we can, so that we can work off the beaten path and through the cracks in the system.

This is the form of wisdom which in many old Pagan traditions was most closely translated as "cunning." The wisdom which looks to create, not just through established channels, but using every tool available.

Now that we've discussed a few different ways of thinking about the divine nature of our Will, let's start to think about how to implement it.

Goals and Intentions

Now that we have learned to *feel* that True Will which springs up out of our bodies; that fire which has the potential to animate our being, it is time to begin to form an intention.

An intention is not just a speculative wish. It is a clear, specific image of precisely what one wants to create. In magic, specificity in intention is very important: you must ask for exactly what you want, including specifying what you *don't* want, or you will not get it.

We have spent previous chapters exploring things you *might* want, entertaining possibilities. Now we are going to begin deciding on *goals*.

These can be as large or as small as you like. The important thing is that they come from within you, from the wellspring of your joy. The other important thing is that they pertain only to *you*. Setting goals to attract friends, partners, collaborators, etc. are perfectly fine goals; but you *don't* want to set a goal which requires a *specific individual* to act according to your plan. This is because each person has their own spark of the Divine.

As we have discussed, consent, boundaries, and autonomy are important for each *individual*, which is why it's generally a terrible idea to try to force or magic another person into behaving as you'd like them to. At that point you are, as one author once put it, "asking the gods to play favorites"—and they might not be too happy about you asking them to privilege your Will over another person's divine calling.

There is a good chance, as difficult as this is to face, that many of the people who are with you at the end of your journey will not be the same ones who were with you at the beginning. People grow and change, and they *especially* grow and change when they are actively reframing the way they think about the world in order to make new things possible. When people grow and change they are sometimes not each others' best-suited friends and partners anymore.

Sometimes they are. But sometimes they're not. And one of the biggest things I see holding people back is fear of losing someone's friendship, or partnership, or disapproval if they pursue autonomy. When I first began therapy, my list of the things that I felt I could not possibly do was dictated almost entirely by what I felt would make my friends, partners, and family members unhappy.

I wasn't wrong; many of them *were* very unhappy with me for a while. Many who had come to depend on me playing certain roles in our relationship were scared. Some no longer speak to me at all. Some have blocked me on all forms of social media. Some expressed the feeling that I "betrayed our community" or "abandoned them" by moving away to pursue things I couldn't get in my hometown.

And some of my old friends grew, in part because me growing required *them* to grow by changing up our social dynamic. And we are much faster and deeper friends now than we were then. Our relationships are immeasurably *better* than they would be if I had not begun to demand better, and to follow my bliss.

There is a time for weaving, for sticking by each other through thick and thin, for building community. And there is a time for the fire to consume what does not serve, to dismantle the old and replace it with the new. There is only so much that can be built, only so much that can grow, if old growth is never cleared away.

Now that we have clarified how and why a spell should *not* depend on another person following your Will (and that did warrant several paragraphs—witches see people trying to do magic about *other* people's lives so regularly that my editor asked me to put this in *twice*), what *should* an intention leading up to spellwork include?

Determine What You Really Want

In her book "The Witch's Eight Paths of Power," Lady Sable Aradia gives some excellent exercises for how to develop one's aptitude for spellwork. The first, and arguably most important discussion she has, is about forming one's intention. She describes why it is important to ask the question "what do I really want?" because if you ask for something that will not satisfy your True Will, you just might get it.[1]

If you think that you want a promotion at your job, *why* do you want that? Is your real goal money, prestige, or power? The ability to make a specific kind of difference in the world? If you can determine what it is you *really* want that is driving your desire for a promotion, you may be able to find a more direct and reliable path to that benefit than simply getting promoted. We all know, after all, that all jobs are a mixed bag, and you wouldn't want to get into the job title you've had your eye on and then realize it did not deliver what you'd hoped for.

Similar logic can be applied to those aspiring to fame, or to artistic careers. What is it that you really want out of that path? We all know that fame, like any job title, is a mixed bag. You could potentially end up accomplishing what you *thought* you wanted, and find that it does not satisfy your true desire. I'll tell you my own story in this respect.

Growing up, my ambition was always to be a science fiction author (this is still an ambition of mine, but it has taken a back seat to my spiritual work for reasons that will soon become obvious). I wanted to help people inhabit vivid new worlds and intimately explore the limits of what was possible.

My science fiction concepts, when they began to blossom, always involved testing our ideas of right and wrong. My stories frequently began with an "antagonist" who was initially assumed to be monstrous and criminal, but who the reader eventually came to side with after learning more about the situation and concluding that the "monster" was actually the one who was doing what needed to be

---

1. Aradia, S. (2014). *The Witch's Eight Paths of Power: A Complete Course in Magick and Witchcraft*. Weiser Books.

done to prevent a greater evil.

Does this sound familiar to anyone? My initial inclination toward science fiction, it turned out, was because it was science fiction that had allowed me to seriously consider ideas which were not permitted by the church I grew up in. In the pages of science fiction books, I had encountered religions with different values from those I'd been raised with, alternative relationship styles, and what I now recognized as *higher* levels of ethics than those I was taught, which were being written by authors who had seriously considered the implications of ideas about social progress and the equality of all beings.

I wanted to help people experience new worlds. I wanted to expose them to ideas which, in my judgment, were *better* than those found in mainstream culture. I didn't really want to be a science fiction author, not at my core. That was just the only way I knew to accomplish those goals. And I *did* in fact get what I asked for; within two years of my first Breaking of Bonds I won one of the most prestigious writing contests in the speculative fiction genre, only to find that the industry was not all I had expected as far as its ability to accomplish my real goals upon becoming an insider.

I now recognize that science fiction is one very effective way to accomplish these goals, and not one I have abandoned completely. But it turned out not to be the most direct path. This book is the most direct path. The work I do in the world, exploring and educating about new worlds and cultures that *really do exist already,* and which you can join and help to build right now, is a more direct path.

For a final example, I'll give the example of love spells. These continue to be one of the most popular reasons people take an interest in magic, and they are...dicey, for reasons we'll discuss shortly. Some people do perfectly well and get exactly what they want with love spells, but these must be considered and constructed carefully to avoid serious complications arising from the ethical problems of trying to impose your own Will on another.

If you are someone who is considering a love spell, I would ask you this: *why?* What is it that you believe you will have or experience if you obtain your ideal partner? Are there, perhaps, more direct and more stable ways of obtaining those things that do not require relying on another person?

This question is especially important because our society often glorifies romance to the point that it becomes a lot like a drug commercial. We are promised all of these things we will be able to feel and do, we are promised that we will meet society's standards for acceptability and success, if we only have the right partner. Too many people enter into relationships almost purely because society has told them that they are a "failure" if they are single, or that romantic love is the only way to true happiness.

These people are often shocked and bitterly disappointed to find that life with a lifelong partner is *not* all they had imagined, or that they are not having luck obtaining romantic love. I would argue that this dynamic is behind the modern phenomena of the angry "incel," who believes that all of their problems will be solved if they can only obtain the love of one or more attractive sexual partners.

Incels explicitly view sexual and romantic success as both the be-all and end-all of both emotional fulfillment and social success, often writing about how they envision their ideal partner as giving them a boundless, deep, unconditional love *and* about how they feel that the attractiveness of one's partner is a measure of one's social worth and level of success in life.

No wonder these folks are terribly unhappy—they believe that they not only deserve, but are *obligated* by society to procure a smoking hot sexual partner who is also the embodiment of love and compassion.

And if they cannot procure such a partner, they are both having their right to love and affection violated by a cruel and uncaring society, *and* are failures as human beings since they have not been able to procure what they see as being a person's evolutionary purpose in life.

What is probably going on, in reality, is that incels have not figured out how to procure satisfactory amounts of love, understanding, acceptance, confidence, social status, etc. through *any* means, and have incorrectly attributed the lack of these things in their lives solely to their lack of romantic partners.

This also goes a long way toward explaining why they are involuntarily celibate, because no sane person will go on a date with someone if they get the sense that they will be expected to supply all of the great many things that are missing from this person's life single handedly.

I hope this extreme example helps those who are longing for romantic love to consider *why* they are longing for it? Is a romantic partner necessarily the most direct or secure route to obtaining social support, affection, and acceptance? Are they necessarily the most direct and secure route to feeling worthy and confident and successful in life?

I would argue that romance is not the most direct or secure way to secure *most* of the things people commonly cite as reasons why they are unhappy being single. There are times when obtaining the right partner really *is* the most direct and secure route to accomplish your goal. But if you undertake a romantic endeavor looking for something that no romantic partner can truly provide for you, you may realize after committing to a relationship that it isn't giving you what you want.

An' It Harm None

I will close with one last caveat offered by Aradia which I very much agree with: it's a good idea to append all magic spells with "an' it harm none," with very few exceptions. Another variant is "if it be for the highest good of all involved."

Aradia herself, for example, attributes her husband's missing limb to a poorly worded money spell in which she and her husband did not specify what the acceptable side effects were to the procurement of money. Turned out, her husband's life insurance policy would pay $100,000 for an amputated limb. They got the money. They did not get what they wanted most.

Another common type of example of "you should have specified" is the all-too common matter of the love spell or cord cutting attempted on somebody else's behalf, which ends up having catastrophic consequences because it turns out that the change the magic was asked to bring about was not actually for the highest good of the people involved.

There are situations in which it is arguable that this caveat is *not* needed. Another famous anecdote that circulates is that of a coven of witches who performed a ritual to put an end to a local serial killer's reign of terror. A few days later, a man who turned out to, in fact, be the serial killer was killed in a car crash. In this situation, it is arguable that the greater good *could* include somebody dying.

There are schools of magic which are fiercely protective of the power of magic to allow the powerless to fight back against the powerful, but even in those cases I recommend a careful consideration of the terms due to the law of unintended consequences.

The topic of how to deal with abusers arises often in my Pagan communities. Unfortunately, we live in a world where it is not uncommon for somebody to be aware of a person who is being violently abusive toward others, and who, for whatever reason, does not seem vulnerable to legal prosecution. This is, in my experience, the most common reason why hexes are invoked.

Even with hexes, I recommend careful formulation so that the act of disempowering the abuser does not accidentally make life *worse* for their victims. There is, after all, the "kick the dog" effect in which abusers can become *more* violent toward their victims as they suffer misfortunes, taking their anger at the world out on those they have power over. This is why the most often prescribed spells for these sorts of situations are spells called "freezer spells," which are designed to "freeze" the abuser's ability to further affect the lives of those around them, or "mirror spells," which are designed to reflect their own actions toward others back on themselves.

Now that we have covered some common "dos" and "don'ts" of magic, we can be strategic in our magic. Let us move on to considering what magic we will eventually weave.

What Do You Really Want?

Now that we've looked at these diverse examples of "what we really want," I invite you to take a few moments to answer the following questions:

What do I most need or want right now? Is there some basic need that must be met before I can really start thinking about other things?

What would I have if I could have anything in the world? Now, what am I *really* getting out of that situation that I've just imagined? What is the underlying feeling, experience, or impact on the world that that situation is giving me?

We will discuss more specifics of how to obtain certain goals in the chapters to come. But for now, take some time to consider the deeper "why" behind the goals that seem obvious to you.

Chapter Eight

Preparing for the Ritual

Many years ago, around the Spring Equinox, I knew it was time for change in my life. My job wasn't working. My relationships weren't working. My creative life wasn't working. I was stuck.

Loki knows what it's like to be bound. More than that, he particularly *specializes* in breaking things that aren't working, so that wonderful new things can come to fill the space they were taking up.

I don't remember if it was me or Loki who suggested this formula. What I do remember is that the results were remarkable. They were probably so remarkable because I was *so* ready for change; it had taken me years to admit that all these things weren't working, and, by the time I finally did, I was fed up.

I had qualms. I had spent years building up bonds to things that I was now realizing were never going to pay off. Bonds to ideas about my career path and feelings of obligation to my employer. Bonds of relationships and feelings of guilt and obligation, even to people who didn't treat me particularly well. Bonds to fear of the consequences of what would happen if I changed absolutely *anything* in my life.

For change to come, those bonds had to be broken. Fortunately, Loki was all too eager to help. He knows what it's like to be fed up with the existing order.

Theology

Traditional Norse magic, called *seiðr*, is conceptualized as "reweaving the threads of fate." A skilled *völva* or *vitki* could create and rearrange energetic bonds to change fate and the future. The imagery of spinning and weaving with thread was taken so literally that *seiðr* was often considered "women's work," just like the spinning and weaving of actual cloth. It's appropriate, then, that we destroy literal threads, ribbons, or yarn for this magic working.

Loki, of course, is not a weaver. He is a destroyer. Not in the negative sense—every time Loki breaks something in the mythos, the end result is that both the gods and mortals receive something much better than what Loki destroyed.

Loki destroys the original plan to build Valhǫll, and Óðinn gets Valhǫll *and* Sleipnir out of the bargain. Loki destroys Sif's hair, and the gods get *most* of their most powerful tools as a result. Loki steals Iðunn's apples and the pantheon ends up with the apples back *and* a new goddess. Loki destroys the world, and a new, better world rises from the ashes.

So it is in our lives. Yet often in Pagan magic, people "call things in" without clearing anything away. Nothing new can grow in an overgrown field. New magical changes cannot happen in our lives unless something is removed to make room for them.

Loki also knows, of course, about breaking bonds. So, instead of weaving bonds of energy and threads of fate in this ritual, we'll be destroying them.

Practice: The Glass Bubble

Now is a good time to practice the glass bubble exercise again as we prepare for the magical work.

When I first began this work with Loki, I was being pulled on by a million threads at all times. I felt obligated to please everyone all the time. I felt that they all needed me. On top of that, I lived in constant fear of total disaster because I'd hit the job market in the worst part of the Great Recession. The threads of guilt, obligation, and anxiety held me immobilized.

This meditation will give you a little more freedom of movement.

Close your eyes and envision all the threads that are pulling on you. In time, you may identify threads that pull you in the direction you *wish* to go, and you may design a bubble that permits only those desired bonds to remain intact. But, when you are first learning your true calling, there is the danger of confusing outside pressures with the calling from within. So, today, let's cut all the threads pulling on you from outside so that what is within can shine forth.

Take a few more deep breaths to center yourself in your body. Begin to imagine a glass bubble materializing around you, glowing gently with your energy.

As it solidifies, the bubble cuts every single thread of expectation or obligation that was pulling on you from outside yourself.

As the threads fall limp, you are free to sit up straighter, free of burdens or bonds.

See how you feel now. See what you *want* now that the bonds are cut. You may be surprised to feel like a completely new and much truer version of yourself.

You can stay in this state for as long as you like.

You can perform this exercise anytime, anywhere, as often as you like.

Some bonds you will surely choose to preserve, re-establish, and perhaps even strengthen. Let this exercise help you ensure that the bonds that guide you and hold you in place are of your free and conscious choosing, not imposed without your consent.

You can even examine individual bonds that you see pulling on your body when you perform this meditation. This can be an excellent way of discovering what in your life is exerting subconscious pressures on life. Such pressures often affect our bodies as well as our actions, and we can sometimes address problems with our actions by working within our bodies or vice versa.

What you learn from examining the bonds you find can help to highlight which choices you make help you to feel better or worse. Paying attention to these sensations can help us to see where boundaries need to be set around activities or experiences that are holding you back, and where physical exercises such as yoga or dance may be useful.

When you decide it is time to break a recurring bond for good, the following ritual can help.

Identify the Bonds You Wish to Break

You came to this work because you felt there was something holding you back. This can be an emotion, belief, attachment, trauma, or situation you are ready to let go of.

For me, when I came to this work I was ready to change everything about my life. That's not unusual; last time I facilitated this work for a coven, I think about a third of the participants had moved to a new state within the year.

But people also come for more subtle reasons. To unbind themselves from their ancestral fears and traumas; to unbind themselves from behaviors they wish to cease. To unbind themselves from, yes, relationships that they have realized are only causing them harm.

It took me many years to fully understand why I needed to break the bonds that I broke back in the spring of 2015. There were things in my environment that were obviously not ideal: a great many people making demands on me, who I had finally realized would never be able to return my support. An entire town of people who had certain expectations of me, developed when I was very young. A job that I had realized I could not stay in any longer and had no wish to advance in.

In hindsight, I understand how I could have exerted more control over those situations if I had had more knowledge. If I'd known more about consent and boundaries, perhaps I could have said "no" to those who made unhealthy demands of me. If I had understood that it was alright to disappoint people's nonconsensual expectations of me, perhaps I could have been who I was while staying in place. If I had known more about business and finance, perhaps I could have started my writing career without leaving.

Perhaps. But on the other hand, we know that invalidating environments are maybe the most important source of emotional distress and dysregulation leading to disempowerment. If it is hard to say "no" to one person who has unhealthy expectations of you, how much harder is it to say "no" to all the ones you live with?

One of the most common pieces of advice I give to those who come to me in distress, to this day, is "move out." It is almost impossible to cultivate good mental health and personal power if you are surrounded by people who invalidate you and make unhealthy demands of you in your own home.

I share these reflections in case they may resonate with you. Our society is full of cautionary tales of people who run from their problems, but don't learn the skills and mindsets to prevent them from happening again. And yet, our society is also full of people who are finding it impossible to follow their bliss, their True Will, their soul contract, because they are surrounded by people who demand things of them.

Now that we've had this discussion, take some time to meditate on what it is you need to unbind yourself from. Which beliefs, emotions, or physical circumstances are holding you back or keeping you in distress? Which conversations or senses of obligation make you contract inside when you bow to them? How can you liberate yourself, by changing your behavior or your circumstances?

One thing about magical work is that it doesn't work *only* on the physical plane. I am a big believer in doing the physical work to give the metaphysical an opportunity to manifest, but these rituals, once they are set in motion, are like freight trains. When I have done serious workings like this one to set my intentions into reality, not all of the events that have happened to bring them to fruition have been physically caused by me. And there has sometimes been a sense that I couldn't stop them from coming to fruition if I *tried*.

I am not saying this to scare you. I am saying this to reassure you. After you do this work, things will happen which will facilitate your freedom. But they might not be what you expect, and you might have to look at them sideways to see the opportunities for what they are.

And you want to be very, very sure of what you want.

Think about it.

Feel it in your body.

Do you know what behaviors, beliefs, emotions, or circumstances you want to be free of?

Okay. Good.

Let's cut the cord.

Identify What You Want to Take Away

In recent years, I have added a new item to my list of ritual ingre-
dients. There has always been a ribbon or a slip of paper to represent
the bond you are breaking. But a couple of years ago, I felt called to
add something else: a second ribbon or cord, to represent what you
want to take away from the ritual. You can also use a piece of jewelry
or another type of item that you procure specifically for this purpose.

The second ribbon is a reminder. It's something you can wear as
a bracelet, if you want to. Like the proverbial string tied around the
finger so that every time the owner notices it they'll be reminded of
something important. The second ribbon is a tangible manifestation
of the work you did in the ritual.

What would you like to take away from the ritual, in place of what
you left behind? What idea, emotion, action, or circumstance would
you like to replace the one you're getting rid of with?

Choose it. Imagine it. Let the feeling of this new reality feel your
body. Let every cell in your nervous system get to know what it feels
like; get to know it intimately. When you have your second ribbon,
you'll imbue all of that feeling into it.

You can "charge" your item with the whole-body memory of this
new thing you are bringing into the world to replace the thing you
want to let go of. In this way, you can access this experience whenever
you like. Whenever you need a resource, or a reminder, or motivation.
You can let it go someday, when and if you're ready to replace this
reality with something new.

Now, let's make sure you have everything you will need for the ritual.

Ritual Materials

This ritual is a variant of what is sometimes called a cord-cutting, or a laying down of burdens and bonds. I've found it interesting to learn that similar rituals are used in different cultures to liberate oneself from a variety of obstacles.

Materials to participate in the ritual:

1. A candle. If it's not safe for you to use real fire, this isn't strictly necessary. An electric candle will also help to stimulate the necessary brain activity.

2. A destructible symbol of the bond(s) you will break. You can write out or draw your bonds on a slip of paper or use a ribbon or thread that seems appropriately symbolic to represent your tie to the negative influence.

3. A symbol of the new reality you want to take away from this ritual. This can be a ribbon or cord for poetic resonance, or a slip of paper if you want to write on it. Or it can be a more permanent object. The important thing is that it be an object you have procured *specifically for this ritual*. If it's an object that is already full of energies and associations, the new energy you put into it could become diluted and less clear when you try to access it in the future.

4. A cutting implement. To be quite honest, I recommend scissors. Knives are more romantic, but they are also considerably less graceful.

5. If desired, a cauldron or other fire-safe container in which to burn the remnants of the bond. This step is cathartic but unnecessary, so it's better to skip it than to use a non-fire-safe container and have it explode.

I recommend that you lay out all of these items in a safe, clean space where you will not be disturbed. Cleanse the place energetically if that is an option. The clearer the local energies are, the more clearly the energies you create will speak to your body.

Once your tools are arrayed in a way that is safe, comfortable, and easy to access, let us begin.

Chapter Nine

The Ritual

The ritual itself, like all rituals, is a moment of decision. It is a moment when we commit to making a metaphysical change whose consequences we may not always be able to reverse or control. So many people do magic because, for a wise magician, this is usually a good thing. I have put intentions out into the universe through rituals which have served me throughout my life.

But it's also okay to back away. One tenant I have learned from rain crowe is the importance of "choosingness," of encouraging a person's freedom of choice up to and including in their level of participation in your spiritual work. I have seen people prepare for the ritual and then decide at the last moment that they weren't ready to break that particular bond yet.

If it gets up to the last moment and it doesn't feel right, that's okay. Maybe it's not the right bond to sever; not the one that is really holding you back.

For those of us who are going to go ahead with the ritual, I want to remind you of the rules that exist to keep everyone safe.

Rules for the Ritual

1. Do NOT attempt to break bonds for someone else unless they have asked you to do so of their own accord. If they are not the ones choosing to make the change, the results could be disastrous. This ritual results in the loss of a major part of one's spiritual ecosystem; a person who is not prepared and who does not desire the change may not be prepared to deal with that change in a healthy way. Horror stories of unintended consequences from people who tried to "help" loved ones by severing their ties to another person or an aspect of their lives abound.Only breaking your own bonds will empower you to manifest your purpose and become who you are meant to be. If you feel that you must change someone else's behavior to empower yourself, that, in itself, is the sign of an unhealthy bond between you and that person. Consider breaking your own bond of attachment to that person's outcomes – to the point that you are willing to consider doing something that affects them without their consent – instead of breaking their bond to someone or something else.It is worth considering with whom the bond originates. Is the other person actively trying to exert influence on you, or are you feeling bound up in their life or situation, even though they have not asked you to be?

2. Use your intuition to determine what bonds you are ready to break. Be precise in your wording. Loki (and magic in general) is renowned for being legalistic and gets more mileage out of using misleading language than out of actually lying. So, let's learn from his bag of tricks and *be precise* in stating what we want.What do you want freedom from? Is it an emotion?

A fear? A reflex? You may wish, and may choose, to do magic to cause changes in physical situations, relationships, and more. However, doing magic that impacts your own internal state will actually be much *more* powerful because your internal state is the only thing you take with you everywhere you go. It dictates your abilities in every situation that crosses your path.

3. Everyone entering the circle for this ritual should absolutely be respectful of all others at all times. This includes deities. Loki should be the only deity formally invited, as he is the one who facilitates this ritual. Toasting rounds may be held for community members to honor all those who have supported them after the ritual. This ritual can be done solitary but doing it with a few trusted friends can enhance its power through their witnessing of your magic. Friends may choose to break bonds in each other's sight so that they can continue to support each other in their growth and liberation.

4. What is shared in the circle STAYS in the circle. Many people choose to break bonds with abusers, employers, or share sensitive information about themselves in the ritual circle. For this reason, I recommend *not* recording this ritual if you are going to conduct it publicly or in a group. I have specifically asked that conferences where I present this ritual not record it for this reason. If the participants cannot speak their uncensored truth aloud, the ritual will be less effective. Since the consequences of certain truths being shared outside the circle can be severe for the individuals who share them, we don't share them beyond the circle. I encourage you to speak your intentions aloud, even if you are conducting the ritual

alone. There really is a difference between what is spoken aloud, and what is merely thought.

What To Expect from The Ritual

This ritual is serious business. A year after performing it for the first time, I had ended several long-term relationships (or rather, the other party chose to end them after I stopped giving them what they demanded of me), and I was living in a different state, working in a different career.

The results were positive — but they were not painless. Money was a real struggle in the first few years of my new career. I accrued medical debts and at one point completely ran out of cash. I was single for nearly five years. In the words of my mentor, "[my] adrenal glands were tested like never before." But, you know what? It was the best thing that ever happened to me. Now, putting my plan to change *everything* in my life into action required real-world preparation. I gave myself a timeline of one year. One year to start working my new career part-time on top of my current job and build up enough savings and clients so that I wouldn't immediately die. One year to procure the training and certifications I needed to make a living. One year to figure out where I was living next and that it was somewhere reasonably far away from the people in my life who were in the habit of guilt-tripping and controlling me.

The beginning of a new year isn't the end of a journey; it's the beginning. But forward motion is possible. Actualizing those plans is possible because *the bonds that stop us from making change are already broken.*

The Speaking Parts

I encourage people performing this ritual to speak their decision to break their bonds aloud, if they can find a place where it is safe to do so. This helps get us in the habit of really acting on our decisions, rather than confining our true self to our internal thoughts.

When organizing this ritual for a group, I invite participants to speak their decision each in turn. I ask people to limit the length of their speaking parts so that the whole group can complete the ritual and speak their truth within one hour.

After the ritual, I advise that food and time for socializing be provided, to allow people to refuel and share social support after expending what can sometimes be a great deal of energy. Protein and hydration can be especially important for people after performing intense energetic or magical work. Receiving supportive physical touch, such as holding hands or hugging can also be particularly helpful.If you wish to participate, I highly recommend that you have a symbol of your bond(s) on hand and that you ritually destroy them when you are done speaking.

I use the following formula when speaking my own breaking of bonds, which may be useful to you:

  1. Prayer of gratitude. It's hard to move forward without support, and those who support us deserve to be honored. For me, this, of course, includes Loki. Other deities, spirits, and mentors may also be honored as seems appropriate to you. Never feel obligated to thank or express gratitude for someone if it doesn't feel right.

  2. Declaration of the breaking. We will not speak in terms of

wishes or hopes. We will speak as though our intention is already a reality — because it is. The bonds of fear, shame, guilt, and all specific obstacles are broken.Of note: If you get there and DON'T feel ready to announce the breaking of a particular bond, that's okay. It may be that you are not yet prepared for the changes the breaking of the bonds would bring.

3. After you have declared the bonds you have broken, ritually destroy the symbol of them by cutting, tearing, burning (etc.) in a manner that is safe for you.

4. PLEASE MAKE SURE YOU COMPLETELY DOUSE AND EXTINGUISH ALL FLAMES BEFORE LEAVING THE RITUAL AREA.

Loki likes fire and he likes mischief. No one has ever gotten hurt, but we've had several small fires as a result of incompletely extinguished flames when conducting this ritual over the years.

Once you have completed the ritual, be gentle with yourself for a while. The nervous system requires rest and nourishment, and social support if it is available, in order to grow and build strength for your next endeavor.

I encourage you to use this ritual and share it with others. This ebook is free to everyone who joins my mailing list, and the mailing list exists primarily so that I can keep folks in the loop around new additions to my healing work. The support groups to which members of my mailing list are invited will remain free for as long as I have the seating capacity to offer free spots.

I am honored that you have chosen to come with me on this journey, and I hope this book will continue to help you grow.

Chapter Ten

The Cycles of Creation

Many Pagan myths portray creation as a cycle. The Norse myths from which Loki hails are arguably one of these. The world is created and populated. The beauties and struggles of the Divine manifesting itself are played out. And, eventually, the time comes for the old world to end, to make room for something new to be created.

Tricksters are often regarded as agents of creation and destruction. In tricksters we see the two as two sides of the same coin: the new thing could not have been created if the old thing had not been destroyed, or if the plans of the established order had gone off without a hitch, or if the rules had been followed. Tricksters are the ones who break the rules, defy the established order, and destroy old growth when there is no room for new growth.

I am closing on this note because, to me, everything about the trickster is important. This is why I work with Loki, and why Papa Legba seems particularly fond of me.

In establishing a new order, it is too easy to get caught up in the feeling that the new order is superior. That the new rules you have set must never be broken, that the new thing you have envisioned must never change. It is too easy to trend toward the image of the glorious liberator, the one who is Good and therefore is not to be defied or disobeyed. See: most revolutionary leaders in human history.

Tricksters are the necessary check on this sort of power. Tricksters remain always in the space of volatility and unacceptability, because that space is a needed safeguard. For as long as there is space to celebrate the unacceptable, there is space to discuss whether standards of acceptability are *right*. For as long as there is volatility, there is the opportunity for innovation. For as long as there is an element of danger, there is space to learn to defend oneself.

As you move into a new cycle, it will be tempting to make rules. And these rules might easily be a good idea. But keep in mind that the time will likely come for the rules to change. That is not failure; that is growth.

As you move into a new cycle, it is likely that you will encounter unexpected obstacles. I have come to see these as gifts. If I had not encountered the obstacles I did, I would be much less powerful than I am today.

And it is, after all, the tricksters who will tell you not to take any bullshit when the world is telling you otherwise.

I opened with an anecdote from a Vodou Fete although Vodou is not my primary tradition, and I'd like to close with one as well. A few hours after Papa Legba exhorted me to stop voluntarily tolerating that which is harmful to me, Papa Gede, a lwa of death and fertility, of destruction and creation, was asked a question by another in attendance.

"What," the young man asked, "is revolution?"

Papa Gede raised a hand to stop the music and call for silence.

"Revolution," Papa Gede said in a thundering voice, "is when you put your foot down and say, 'No. I have had enough.' Revolution is when you do not do as you are told."

Papa Gede, I realized, was the perfect person to ask about revolution. Especially given the legacy of the Haitian Revolution, often considered the most successful revolution and move to self-governance by self-liberated slaves in recorded history.

The revolutionary movements of today have decidedly mixed feelings on many matters, and are a good example of the danger of the "glorious liberator who must not be questioned." I have been criticized by some of them for promoting personal empowerment, which some of them see as being contrary to communal empowerment. I have been criticized by some for the very endeavor of "Breaking Your Bonds" on the basis that we rise together, not separately.

But other revolutionaries are in agreement with me on a few things. Individual acts of rebellion and personal liberation, they say, are revolutionary. Cultivating the ability to say "no," and to ask for what we really want, are revolutionary. There is a time for collective action and a time for loyalty. But before new connections, communities, and codes of ethics can be created, the old ones must often be escaped. Saying "no" to your comrade who proposes something you know to be wrong is just as important as saying "no" to someone who is openly engaging in oppression.

Papa Gede illustrates this point by testing the young man who has asked him this question. He commands him to smoke a cigar each day for seven days in order to gain wisdom.

When the young man agrees, Papa Gede frowns. That was the wrong answer. Papa Gede didn't want him to follow orders; he wanted him to say "no," to stand up for himself. Gods test us this way, sometimes.

"You humans waste so much time doing what you are told," Papa

Gede declared, then took a swig from one of the rum bottles that had been offered to him on the altar.

"You will have to unlearn a great deal, because your schools are designed to teach compliance. Being alive is not about doing what you are told," Papa Gede continued. "To be alive is to have divine potential. Potential to change things. You do not come into the world to let it shape you; you come into the world in order to shape *it*."

A better world is being born as you read these words. The pains of destruction are the labor pains of the new world being born. No birth is easy or clean or pleasant. It's bloody, screaming, desperate work where sometimes the laboring person wants to give up. But at the end, something new is made. Something that was utterly impossible before.

What impossible thing will you create?

Acknowledgements

This book has been years in the making, dating at least from the time I first began offering facilitation of my Breaking of Bonds ritual to the public. Putting it together was quite an endeavor, as there are so many spokes which seem connected to a central hub. It became clear to me during my work on this book that at least two other books need to follow it: you can expect Book Two, focusing on the practical magic around money, finance, and freedom of movement in 2024.

I'd like to thank Colleen McGee as always for her encouragement, and my editor Izu Spielman for his generous support in getting this book across the finish line. I'd also like to thank Bekka Emerald for being one of my major encouragers about my public work, and Jessica Burch for being my sounding board.

I would also like to thank Emmanuel Dagher and rain crowe for their generous attention and permission to quote them in this book. I am so grateful to have met both of these healers who have shown me the potential of spiritual healing and the diversity of approaches that are possible. I am grateful to Elmo Painter-Edington for showing me the potential of somatic therapy and for the mindfulness circles she led at World Tree Healing.

The entire Loki's Wyrdlings community has helped make this book and its associated services a reality. It was through Loki's Wyrdlings that I first offered a public ritual in 2020 and received such a profound response that I knew I had to keep expanding this work. This book will debut at Loki's Wyrdlings' Loki Fest 2023, where I will be facilitating the Breaking of Bonds ritual thanks to the kind support of Ky Greene and the Loki Fest Committee.

Thanks to Mambo Jae Marie for inviting me into the world of Vodou and her service to the community. I must also thank Rev

Bishop Lisa Gruber and Rev. Bishop L. Delon, D. Div. of the Occult Society for facilitating the Fèt Gede at which I met the lwa I've quoted here.

Last but never least, I must thank the deities who have come to help with this work. Thanks first and foremost to Loki, who remained with me when no other god could reach me. Thanks to the Lady who has kept me on the path I asked for through the most surprising of developments, and to Papa Legba and Papa Gede who serve the Vodou communities with such wise and loving counsel.

I hope this book will benefit you, and I hope to continue offering online ritual facilitation and support groups for years to come. If you haven't already, you can learn more about the events and services I offer by joining my mailing list at CatherineCarr.org.

About the Author

Catherine Carr earned her B.S. in Neuroscience from the University of Michigan and worked in clinical research for five years before becoming a full-time writer and student of the spiritual arts. Her writings on religion and spirituality have appeared in *The Wild Hunt, The Crazy Wisdom Community Journal,* and more.

She became a student of Cherry Hill Seminary and the Village Mystery Temple and Dream School in 2020. She now facilitates free rituals and support groups and offers life coaching from a spiritually-oriented perspective.

CatherineCarr.Org

www.ingramcontent.com/pod-product-compliance
Lightning Source LLC
Chambersburg PA
CBHW061656120626
46550CB00003B/961